Congaree National Park Visitor Study

Spring 2011

Natural Resource Report NPS/NRSS/EQD/NRR— 2012/490

Colleen Kulesza, Yen Le, Steven J. Hollenhorst

Visitor Services Project
Park Studies Unit
University of Idaho
Moscow, ID 83844-1139

February 2012

U.S. Department of the Interior
National Park Service
Natural Resource Stewardship and Science
Fort Collins, Colorado

The National Park Service Natural Resource Stewardship and Science publishes a range of reports that address natural resource topics of interest and applicability to a broad audience in the National Park Service and others in natural resource management, including scientists, conservation and environmental constituencies, and the public.

The Natural Resource Report Series is used to disseminate high-priority, current natural resource management information with managerial application. The series targets a general, diverse audience, and may contain NPS policy considerations or address sensitive issues of management applicability.

All manuscripts in the series receive the appropriate level of peer review to ensure that the information is scientifically credible, technically accurate, appropriately written for the intended audience, and designed and published in a professional manner.

Data in this report were collected and analyzed using methods based on established, peer-reviewed protocols and were analyzed and interpreted within the guidelines of the protocols.

Views, statements, findings, conclusions, recommendations, and data in this report do not necessarily reflect views and policies of the National Park Service, U.S. Department of the Interior. Mention of trade names or commercial products does not constitute endorsement or recommendation for use by the U.S. Government.

This report is available from the Social Science Division (http://www.nature.nps.gov/socialscience/index.cfm) and the Natural Resource Publications Management website (http://www.nature.nps.gov/publications/nrpm/).

This report and other reports by the Visitor Services Project (VSP) are available from the VSP website (http://www.psu.uidaho.edu/reports.htm) or by contacting the VSP office at (208) 885-7863.

Please cite this publication as:

Kulesza, C., Y. Le, & S. J. Hollenhorst. 2012. Congaree National Park visitor study: Spring 2011. Natural Resource Report NPS/NRSS/EQD/NRR—2012/490. National Park Service, Fort Collins, Colorado.

NPS 178/112717, February 2012

Contents

Contents (continued)

Figures

Figures (continued)

Figures (continued)

Tables

Executive Summary

This visitor study report profiles a systematic random sample of Congaree National Park (NP) visitors during May 2–15, 2011. A total of 450 questionnaires was distributed to visitor groups. Of those, 313 questionnaires were returned, resulting in a 69.6% response rate.

Group size and type
Fifty-four percent of visitor groups consisted of two people and 16% were visiting alone. Sixty-four percent of visitor groups consisted of family groups.

State or country of residence
United States visitors were from 40 states and Washington, DC and comprised 94% of total visitation during the survey period, with 54% from South Carolina. International visitors were from 9 countries and comprised 6% of total visitation.

Frequency of visits
Seventy-six percent of visitors visited the park once in the past 12 months and 62% were visiting the park for the first time in their lives. Twenty percent had visited 4 or more times in their lifetime.

Age, ethnicity, race, and educational level
Thirty-three percent of visitors were ages 56-70 years, 28% were 21-40 years old, 12% were ages 15 years or younger, and 5% were 71 or older. Four percent were Hispanic or Latino. Ninety-one percent of visitors were White and 4% were Black or African American. Forty-one percent of respondents had completed a graduate degree and 31% had a bachelor's degree.

Physical conditions
Eight percent of visitor groups had members with physical conditions affecting their ability to access or participate in activities and services.

Awareness of park programs
Fifty-nine percent of visitor groups were aware, prior to their visit, of the various programs offered at the park.

Knowledge of wilderness
Fifty-seven percent of the respondents said they were aware of congressionally designated wilderness before their visit to the park. Forty-six percent of visitor groups said they learned about wilderness while at the park.

Non-native species management
Fifty-two percent of the respondents were aware of the policy regarding removal of non-native species. Most visitor groups (83%) were in support of removal of non-native plants and 73% were supportive of removal of non-native animals.

Scientific research and education in the park
Forty percent of the visitor groups noticed scientists working or scientific markers or equipment being used in the park. Through programs or products, 25% of the visitors learned about the results of scientific studies conducted at the park.

Information sources
Most visitors (91%) obtained information about the park prior to their visit. Of those visitors, 50% used the park website and 30% obtained their information from friends/relatives/word of mouth.

Park as destination
Seventy-four percent of visitor groups said the park was their primary destination and 21% said it was one of several destinations.

Primary reason for visiting the area
Twenty-nine percent of visitor groups were residents of the area (within 1 hour drive of the park). The most common primary reasons for visiting the park area among non-resident visitor groups were to visit the park (65%) and visit friends/relatives in the area (12%).

Executive Summary (continued)

Overnight stays	Forty percent of visitor groups stayed overnight away from home either in the park or the area. Of those visitors that stayed outside the park within 1-hour drive, 49% stayed 1 night and 21% stayed for 2 nights.
Accommodations	Of those visitor groups that stayed outside the park in the area within 1-hour drive of the park, 83% stayed in a lodge, hotel, motel, vacation rental, or B&B.
Time spent at park and in the area	Fifty percent of visitor groups spent 3 - 4 hours in the park and 36% percent of visitor groups spent 1 - 2 hours. Thirty-nine percent of visitors stayed in the park area (within 1-hour drive) for 1 - 2 hours and 36% spent 3 - 4 hours in the park area. The average length of stay in the park was 6.1 hours. The average length of stay in the area was 38.1 hours, or 1.6 days.
Activities	The most common activities were walking/hiking (82%), visiting the visitor center (71%), and birdwatching (24%).
Use of park trails	The Elevated Boardwalk Trail was used by 81% of the visitor groups and the Low Boardwalk Trail was used by 62%.
Information services and facilities	The information services and facilities most commonly used by visitor groups were the park brochure/map (86%), assistance from park staff (78%), and the visitor center exhibits (74%).
Visitor services and facilities	The visitor services and facilities most commonly used by visitor groups were the boardwalks (89%), restrooms (86%), and parking areas (83%).
Protecting park attributes, resources, and experiences	The highest combined proportions of "extremely important" and "very important" ratings of protecting park attributes, resources, and experiences included native wildlife (90%), natural quiet/sounds of nature (89%), clean water (88%), and clean air (87%).
Elements affecting park experience	Thirty-one percent of visitor groups reported that encountering small numbers of visitors on the trails added to their trip experience. Airplane noise detracted from 12% of the visitor groups' experiences.
Expenditures	The average visitor group expenditure (inside and outside the park within 1-hour drive) was $199. The median group expenditure (50% of groups spent more and 50% of groups spent less) was $55. The majority of expenses were for lodging (30%) and gas and oil (21%). The average total expenditure per capita was $106.
Future visit	Fifty-nine percent of visitor groups were interested in canoeing/kayaking on future visits and 50% were interested in bird walks. Eighty-eight percent of visitor groups were interested in learning more about the park on future visits.
Overall quality	Most visitor groups (95%) rated the overall quality of facilities, services, and recreational opportunities at Congaree NP as "very good" or "good." One percent of groups rated the overall quality as "very poor" or "poor."

For more information about the Visitor Services Project, please contact the Park Studies Unit at the University of Idaho at (208) 885-7863 or the following website http://www.psu.uidaho.edu.

Acknowledgements

We thank Colleen Kulesza for compiling the report, Nancy Holmes and Corinne Fenner for overseeing the fieldwork, Lauren Gurniewicz and the staff and volunteers of Congaree NP for assisting with the survey, and David Vollmer and Matthew Strawn for data processing.

About the Authors

Colleen Kulesza is a doctoral candidate at the University of Idaho and a research assistant for the Visitor Services Project. Yen Le, Ph.D., is Assistant Director of the Visitor Services Project at the University of Idaho, and Steven Hollenhorst, Ph.D., is the Director of the Park Studies Unit, Department of Conservation Social Sciences, University of Idaho.

Introduction

This report describes the results of a visitor study at Congaree National Park (NP) in Hopkins, SC, conducted May 2–15, 2011 by the National Park Service (NPS) Visitor Services Project (VSP), part of the Park Studies Unit (PSU) at the University of Idaho.

As described in the National Park Service website for Congaree National Park: "Welcome to the largest remnant of old-growth floodplain forest remaining on the continent! Experience champion trees, towering to record size amidst astonishing biodiversity…Congaree National Park houses a museum quality exhibit area within the Harry Hampton Visitor Center, a 2.4 mile boardwalk loop trail, over 20 miles of backwoods hiking trails, canoeing, kayaking, fishing and more…As a designated Wilderness area, International Biosphere Reserve, Globally Important Bird Area, and the largest intact tract of old-growth floodplain forest in North America, Congaree National Park is home to a variety of ongoing research and education projects." (http://www.nps.gov/cong/index.htm, retrieved October, 2011)

Organization of the Report

This report is organized into three sections.

Section 1: **Methods**. This section discusses the procedures, limitations, and special conditions that may affect the study results.

Section 2: **Results**. This section provides a summary for each question in the questionnaire and includes visitor comments to open-ended questions. The presentation of the results of this study does not follow the order of questions in the questionnaire.

Section 3: **Appendices**

Appendix 1: *The Questionnaire*. A copy of the questionnaire distributed to visitor groups.

Appendix 2: *Additional Analysis*. A list of sample questions for cross-references and cross comparisons. Comparisons can be analyzed within a park or between parks. Results of additional analyses are not included in this report.

Appendix 3: *Decision rules for checking non-response bias*. An explanation of how the non-response bias was determined.

Presentation of the Results

Results are represented in the form of graphs (see example below); scatter plots, pie charts, tables and text.

SAMPLE

1. The figure title describes the graph's information.

2. Listed above the graph, the "N" shows the number of individuals or visitor groups responding to the question. If "N" is less than 30, "**CAUTION!**" is shown on the graph to indicate the results may be unreliable.

   * appears when the total percentages do not equal 100 due to rounding.

   ** appears when total percentages do not equal 100 because visitors could select more than one answer choice.

3. Vertical information describes the response categories.

4. Horizontal information shows the number or proportion of responses in each category.

5. In most graphs, percentages provide additional information.

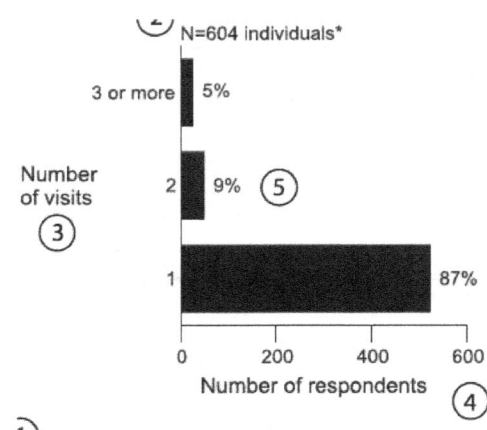

Methods

Survey Design and Procedures

Sample size and sampling plan

All VSP questionnaires follow design principles outlined in Don A. Dillman's book *Mail and Internet Surveys: The Tailored Design Method* (2007). Using this method, the sample size was calculated based on park visitation statistics of previous years.

Brief interviews were conducted with a systematic, random sample of visitor groups that arrived at the visitor center during May 2–15, 2011. Visitors were surveyed between the hours of 8 a.m. and 5 p.m. During this survey, 456 visitor groups were contacted and 450 of these groups (98.7%) accepted questionnaires. (The average acceptance rate for 228 VSP visitor studies conducted from 1988 through 2010 is 91.5%.) Questionnaires were completed and returned by 313 respondents, resulting in a 69.6% response rate for this study. (The average response rate for the 228 VSP visitor studies is 72.6%)

Questionnaire design

The Congaree National Park questionnaire was developed at a workshop held with park staff to design and prioritize questions. Some of the questions were comparable with VSP studies conducted at other parks while others were customized for Congaree NP. Many questions asked visitors to choose answers from a list of responses, often with an open-ended option, while others were completely open-ended.

No pilot study was conducted to test the Congaree NP questionnaire. However, all questions followed Office Management and Budget (OMB) guidelines and/or were used in previous surveys; thus, the clarity and consistency of the survey instrument have been tested and supported.

Survey procedure

Visitor groups were greeted, briefly introduced to the purpose of the study, and asked to participate. If visitors agreed, they were asked which member (at least 16 years old) had the next birthday. The individual with the next birthday was selected to complete the questionnaire for the group. An interview, lasting approximately two minutes, was conducted with that person to determine group size, group type, age of the member completing the questionnaire, and how this visit to the park fit into their group's travel plans. These individuals were asked their names and addresses, and telephone numbers or email addresses in order to mail a reminder/thank-you postcard and follow-ups. Participants were asked to complete the questionnaire after their visit, and return it in the Business Reply Mail envelope provided.

Two weeks following the survey, a reminder/thank-you postcard was mailed to all participants who provided a valid mailing address (see Table 1). Replacement questionnaires were mailed to participants who had not returned their questionnaires four weeks after the survey. Seven weeks after the survey, a second round of replacement questionnaires was mailed to participants who had not returned their questionnaires.

Table 1. Follow-up mailing distribution

Mailing	Date	U.S.	International	Total
Postcards	May 23, 2011	423	18	441
1st Replacement	June 7, 2011	198	8	206
2nd Replacement	June 27, 2011	174	0	174

The 2-minute interview was conducted with 450 participants to Congaree National Park. This resulted in 15 hours of participants' time dedicated to the interviews. A total of 313 respondents completed and returned their questionnaire. It is estimated that each questionnaire takes an average of 20 minutes. This resulted in a total of 104 hours of respondents' time dedicated to completing the questionnaire. Respondents dedicated a total of approximately 119 hours of time to provide the data in this report.

Data analysis

Returned questionnaires were coded and the responses were processed using custom and standard statistical software applications—Statistical Analysis Software® (SAS), and a custom designed FileMaker Pro® application. Descriptive statistics and cross-tabulations were calculated for the coded data; responses to open-ended questions were categorized and summarized. Double-key data entry validation was performed on numeric and text entry variables and the remaining checkbox (bubble) variables were read by optical mark recognition (OMR) software.

Limitations

As with all surveys, this study has limitations that should be considered when interpreting the results.

1. This was a self-administered survey. Respondents completed the questionnaire after the visit, which may have resulted in poor recall. Thus, it is not possible to know whether visitor responses reflected actual behavior.

2. The data reflect visitor use patterns at the selected sites during the study period of May 2–15, 2011. The results present a 'snapshot in time' and do not necessarily apply to visitors during other times of the year.

3. Caution is advised when interpreting any data with a sample size of less than 30, as the results may be unreliable. Whenever the sample size is less than 30, the word **"CAUTION!"** is included in the graph, figure, table, or text.

4. Occasionally, there may be inconsistencies in the results. Inconsistencies arise from missing data or incorrect answers (due to misunderstood directions, carelessness, or poor recall of information). Therefore, refer to both the percentage and N (number of individuals or visitor groups) when interpreting the results.

Special conditions

The weather during the survey period was a sunny, warm and humid, interspersed with occasional cool, rainy days. No special events occurred in the area that would have affected the type and amount of visitation to the park.

Checking non-response bias

Five variables were used to check non-response bias: participant age, group size, group type, park as destination, and participant travel distance to the park. All variables were found to be significantly different between respondents and non-respondents (see Tables 2 - 5). The results indicate some biases occurred due to nonresponse. Visitors at younger age ranges (especially 40 and younger), who came from the local area (within 50 miles radius), and visitors traveling with friends were under-represented in the survey results. See Appendix 3 for more details on the non-response bias checking procedures.

Table 2. Comparison of respondents and non-respondents by average age and group size

Variable	Respondents	Non-respondents	p-value (t-test)
Age (years)	50.21 (N=312)	39.29 (N=136)	<0.001
Group size	2.43 (N=307)	2.73 (N=133)	0.027

Table 3. Comparison of respondents and non-respondents by group type

Group type	Respondents	Non-respondents	p-value (chi-square)
Alone	49 (16%)	18 (13%)	
Family	196 (64%)	69 (51%)	
Friends	47 (15%)	34 (25%)	
Family and friends	14 (5%)	11 (8%)	
Other	1 (0.3%)	4 (3%)	
			0.003

Table 4. Comparison of respondents and non-respondents by primary destination

Destination	Respondents	Non-respondents	p-value (chi-square)
Park as primary destination	216 (70%)	113 (84%)	
Park as one of several destinations	74 (24%)	18 (13%)	
Unplanned visit	18 (6%)	4 (3%)	
			0.011

Table 5. Comparison of respondents and non-respondents by distance from home to park

Distance	Respondents	Non-respondents	p-value (chi-square)
Within 50 miles	117 (39%)	76 (57%)	
51-100 miles	30 (10%)	12 (9%)	
101-200 miles	36 (15%)	9 (7%)	
201 miles or more	108 (36%)	32 (24%)	
International visitors	12 (4%)	5 (4%)	
			0.009

Results

Group and Visitor Characteristics

Note: Non-response bias was detected during data analysis; therefore some results should be interpreted with caution. See Appendix 3 for more details on the non-response bias checking procedures.

Visitor group size

Question 19b
On this visit, how many people were in your personal group, including yourself?

Results
- 54% of visitor groups consisted of two people (see Figure 1).

- 16% were alone.

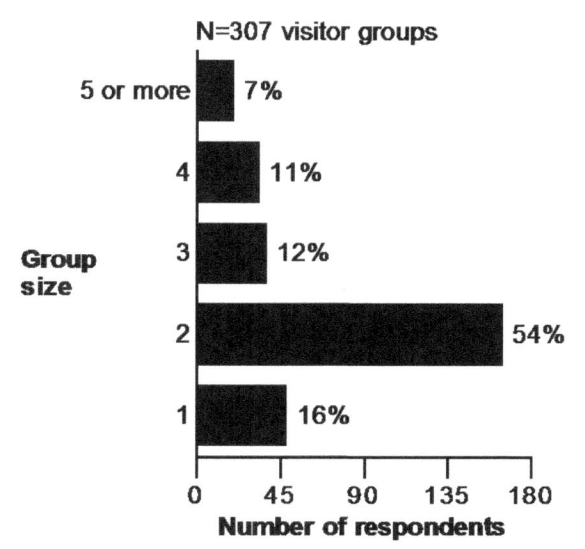

Figure 1. Visitor group size

Visitor group type

Question 19a
On this visit, what kind of personal group (not guided tour/school/other organized group) were you with?

Results
- 64% of visitor groups consisted of family members (see Figure 2).

- No "other" group types (<1%) were specified.

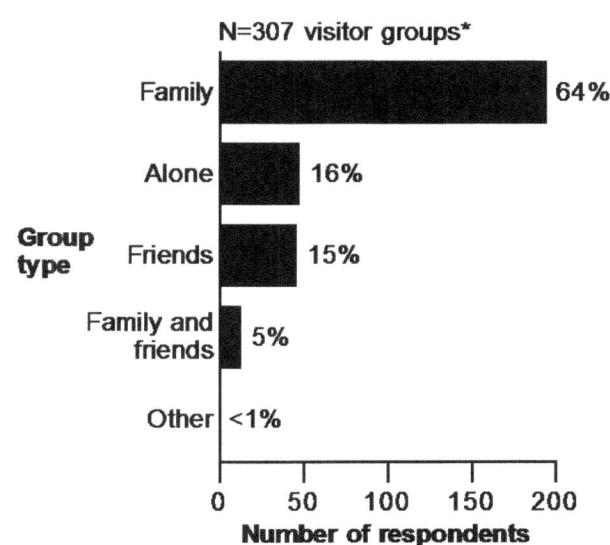

Figure 2. Visitor group type

*total percentages do not equal 100 due to rounding
**total percentages do not equal 100 because visitors could select more than one answer

Visitors with organized groups

Question 18a

On this visit, were you and your personal group with a commercial guided tour group?

Results

- 1% of visitor groups were with a commercial guided tour group (see Figure 3).

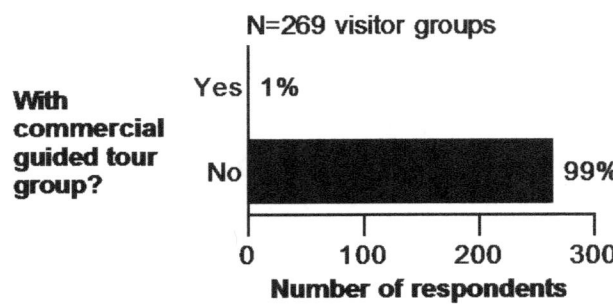

Figure 3. Visitors with a commercial guided tour group

Question 18b

On this visit, were you and your personal group with a school/ educational group?

Results

- 3% of visitor groups were with a school/educational group (see Figure 4).

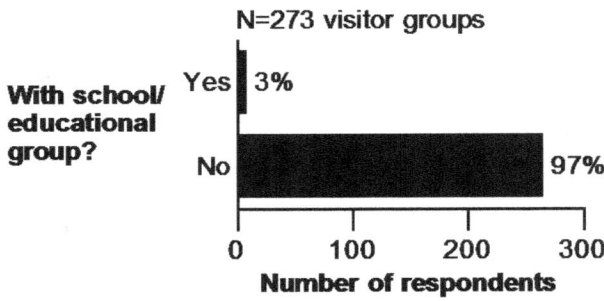

Figure 4. Visitors with a school/educational group

Question 18c

On this visit, were you and your personal group with an "other" organized group (scouts, work, church, etc.)?

Results

- 2% of visitor groups were with an "other" organized group (see Figure 5).

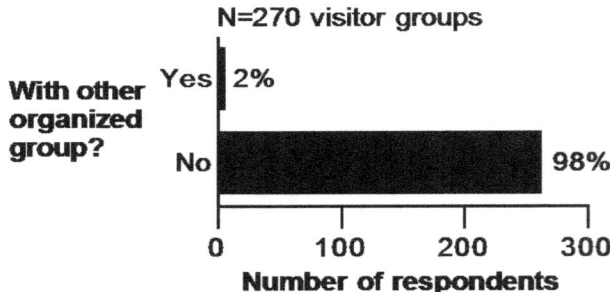

Figure 5. Visitors with an "other" organized group

---

*total percentages do not equal 100 due to rounding

**total percentages do not equal 100 because visitors could select more than one answer

Question 18d

If you were with one of these organized groups, how many people, including yourself, were in this group?

Results – Interpret with **CAUTION!**

- Not enough visitor groups responded to this question to provide reliable results (see Figure 6).

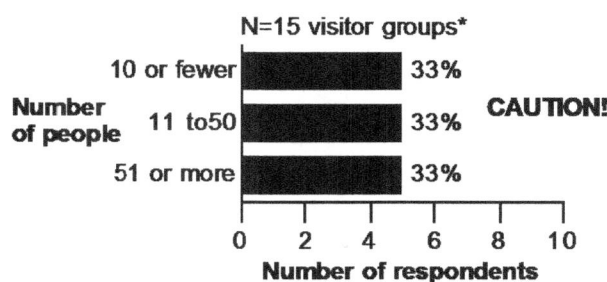

Figure 6. Organized group size

*total percentages do not equal 100 due to rounding
**total percentages do not equal 100 because visitors could select more than one answer

9

United States visitors by state of residence

Question 20b

For you and your personal group on this visit, what is your state of residence?

Note: Response was limited to seven members from each visitor group.

Results
- U.S. visitors were from 40 states and comprised 94% of total visitation to the park during the survey period.

- 54% of U.S. visitors came from South Carolina (see Table 6 and Figure 7).

- 6% came from North Carolina and 5% were from Florida.

- Smaller proportions came from 37 other states and Washington, DC.

Table 6. United States visitors by state of residence

State	Number of visitors	Percent of U.S. visitors N=638	Percent of total visitors N=680
South Carolina	347	54%	51%
North Carolina	41	6%	6%
Florida	32	5%	5%
Pennsylvania	22	3%	3%
Georgia	21	3%	3%
California	19	3%	3%
Ohio	17	3%	3%
Michigan	13	2%	2%
Tennessee	11	2%	2%
Maryland	10	2%	1%
New York	10	2%	1%
29 other states and Washington, DC	95	15%	14%

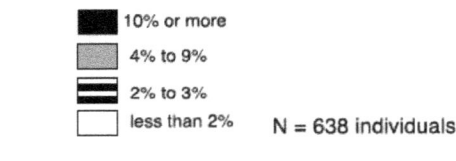

10% or more
4% to 9%
2% to 3%
less than 2%   N = 638 individuals

Hawaii

Congaree National Park

uerto Rico

*total percentages do not equal 100 due to rounding
**total percentages do not equal 100 because visitors could select more than one answer

Figure 7. United States visitors by state of residence
Visitors from South Carolina and adjacent states by county of residence

Note: Response was limited to seven members from each visitor group.

Results

- Visitors from South Carolina and adjacent states were from 49 counties and comprised 66% of the total U.S. visitation to the park during the survey period.

- 34% came from Richland County, SC (see Table 7).

- 22% Came from Lexington County, SC.

- Small proportions of visitors came from 47 other counties in South Carolina and adjacent states.

Table 7. Visitors from South Carolina and adjacent states by county of residence

County, State	Number of visitors, N=420 individuals	Percent*
Richland, SC	141	34
Lexington, SC	92	22
Kershaw, SC	18	4
Greenville, SC	16	4
Charleston, SC	13	3
Buncombe, NC	11	3
Mecklenburg, NC	9	2
Aiken, SC	8	2
Iredell, NC	8	2
Sumter, SC	8	2
Orangeburg, SC	7	2
York, SC	7	2
Oconee, SC	6	1
Blount, TN	5	1
Greenwood, SC	5	1
Cobb, GA	4	1
Gwinnett, GA	4	1
Spartanburg, SC	4	1
Cherokee, GA	3	1
Clarendon, SC	3	1
Florence, SC	3	1
Horry, SC	3	1
Jasper, SC	3	1
Madison, GA	3	1
25 other counties	36	8

*total percentages do not equal 100 due to rounding
**total percentages do not equal 100 because visitors could select more than one answer

International visitors by country of residence

Question 20b

For you and your personal group on this visit, what is your country of residence?

Note: Response was limited to seven members from each visitor group.

Results

- International visitors were from 9 countries and comprised 6% of total visitation to the park during the survey period.

- 31% of international visitors came from Germany (see Table 8).

- 17% were from Australia.

- Smaller proportions of international visitors came from 7 other countries.

Table 8. International visitors by country of residence

Country	Number of visitors	Percent of international visitors N=42*	Percent of total visitors N=680
Germany	13	31	2
Australia	7	17	1
Canada	6	14	1
Italy	4	10	1
India	3	7	<1
The Netherlands	3	7	<1
Austria	2	5	<1
Switzerland	2	5	<1
United Kingdom	2	5	<1

---

*total percentages do not equal 100 due to rounding
**total percentages do not equal 100 because visitors could select more than one answer

Number of visits to Congaree NP in past 12 months

Question 20c

For you and your personal group on this visit, how many times have you visited Congaree NP in the past 12 months (including this visit)?

Note: Response was limited to seven members from each visitor group.

Results

• 76% of visitors visited the park once in the past 12 months (see Figure 8).

• 17% of visitors visited two or three times.

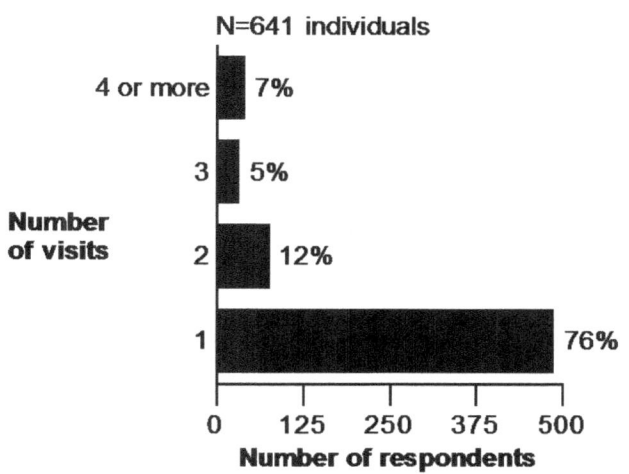

Figure 8. Number of visits to park in past 12 months

Number of lifetime visits to Congaree NP

Question 20d

For you and your personal group on this visit, how many times have you visited Congaree NP in your lifetime (including this visit)?

Note: Response was limited to seven members from each visitor group.

Results

• 62% of visitors were visiting the park for the first time (see Figure 9).

• 20% had visited 4 or more times in their lifetime.

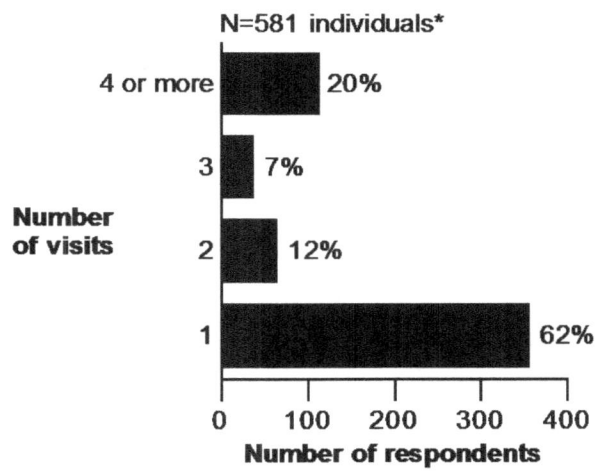

Figure 9. Number of visits to park in lifetime

*total percentages do not equal 100 due to rounding
**total percentages do not equal 100 because visitors could select more than one answer

Number of visits to other national parks in past 12 months

Question 20e
For you and your personal group on this visit, how many times have you visited other national parks in the past 12 months (including this visit)?

Note: Response was limited to seven members from each visitor group.

Results
- 35% of visitors had visited other national parks once in the past 12 months (see Figure 10).

- 25% had visited other national parks 5 or more times.

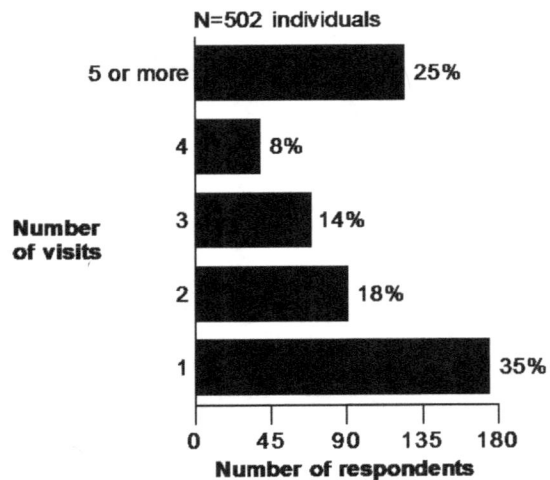

Figure 10. Number of visits to other national parks in past 12 months

Number of lifetime visits to other national parks

Question 20f
For you and your personal group on this visit, how many times have you visited a national park in your lifetime (including this visit)?

Note: Response was limited to seven members from each visitor group.

Results
- 35% of visitors had visited other national parks between 1 and 5 times in their lifetime (see Figure 11).

- 25% had visited other national parks 21 or more times.

- For 9% of visitors, this was their first visit to any national park.

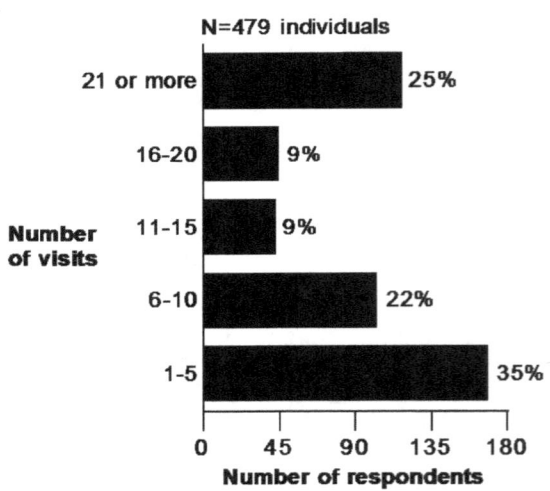

Figure 11. Number of visits to other national parks in lifetime

---

*total percentages do not equal 100 due to rounding
**total percentages do not equal 100 because visitors could select more than one answer

Visitor age

Question 20a

For you and your personal group on this visit, what is your current age?

Note: Response was limited to seven members from each visitor group.

Results

- Visitor ages ranged from 1 to 97 years.

- 33% of visitors were 56 to 70 years old (see Figure 12).

- 28% were 21-40 years old.

- 12% were 15 years old or younger.

- 5% were 71 years or older.

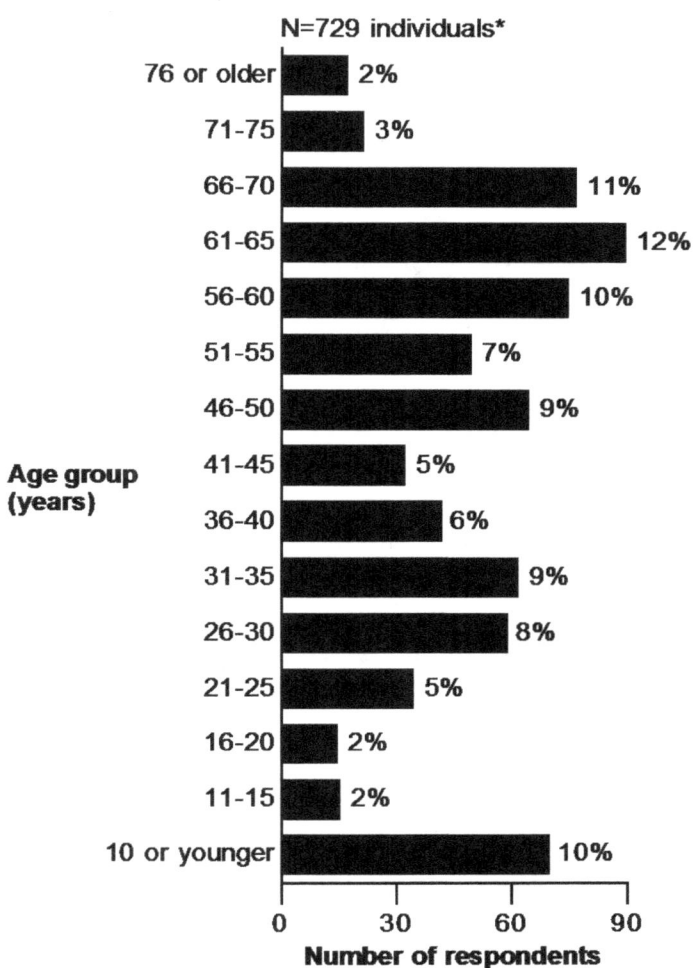

Figure 12. Visitor age

Visitor ethnicity

Question 23a
Are you or members of your personal group Hispanic or Latino?

Note: Response was limited to seven members from each visitor group.

Results
- 4% of visitors were Hispanic or Latino (see Figure 13).

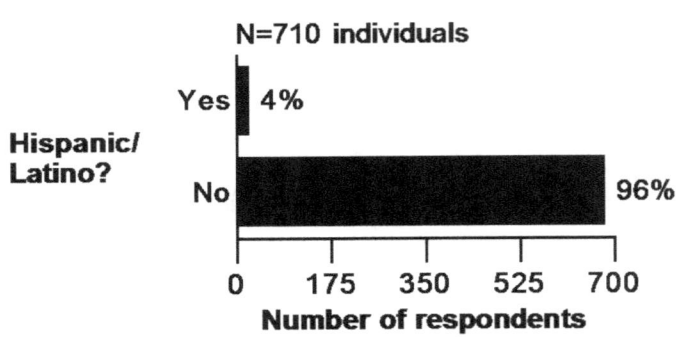

Figure 13. Visitors who were Hispanic or Latino

Visitor race

Question 23b
What is your race? What is the race of each member of your personal group?

Note: Response was limited to seven members from each visitor group.

Results
- 91% of visitors were White (see Figure 14).

- 4% were Black or African American.

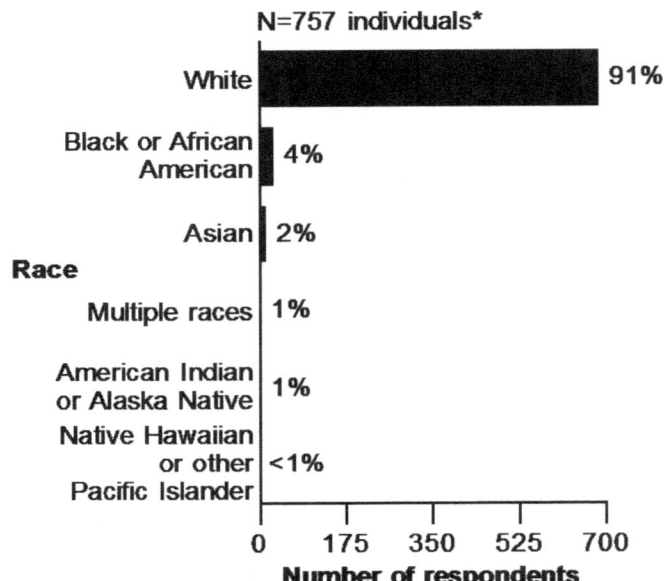

Figure 14. Visitor race

---

*total percentages do not equal 100 due to rounding
**total percentages do not equal 100 because visitors could select more than one answer

Visitors with physical conditions affecting access/participation

Question 22a

Does anyone in your personal group have mobility or other physical impairments?

Results

- 8% of visitor groups had members with physical conditions (see Figure 15).

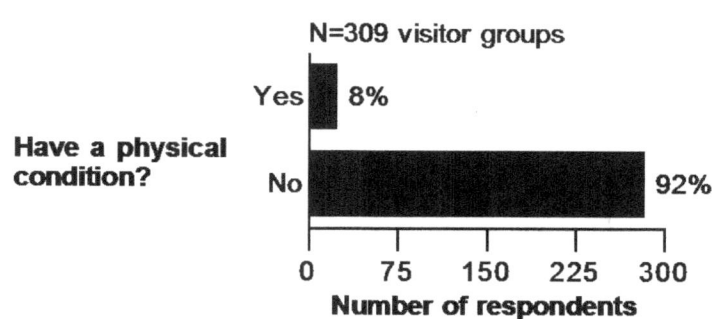

Figure 15. Visitor groups that had members with physical conditions affecting access/participation

Question 22b

If YES, did anyone in your personal group have a physical condition that made it difficult to access or participate in park activities or services?

Results – Interpret with **CAUTION!**

- Not enough visitor groups responded to provide reliable results (see Figure 16).

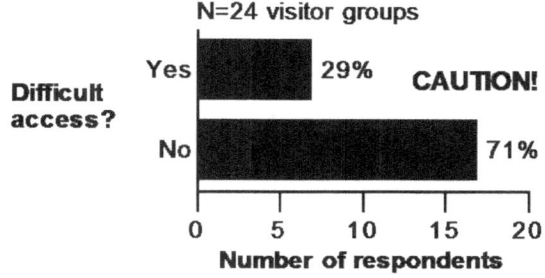

Figure 16. Visitor groups who had a member with difficulties accessing services.

---

*total percentages do not equal 100 due to rounding

**total percentages do not equal 100 because visitors could select more than one answer

Respondent level of education

Question 21

    For you only, what is the highest level of education you have completed?

Results

- 41% of respondents had a graduate degree (see Figure 17).

- 31% of respondents had a bachelor's degree.

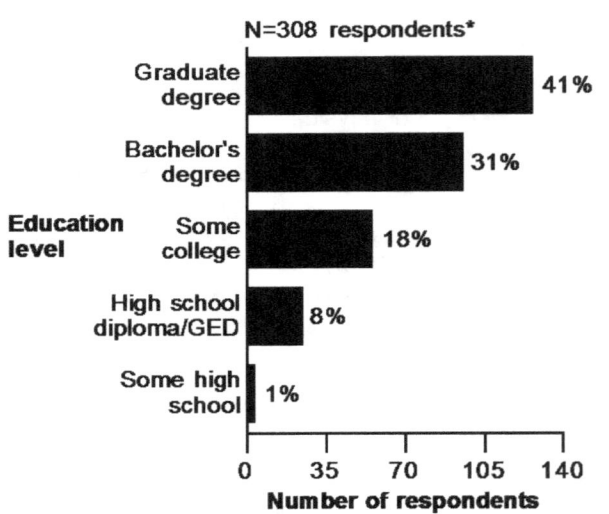

Figure 17. Respondent level of education

---

*total percentages do not equal 100 due to rounding

**total percentages do not equal 100 because visitors could select more than one answer

Household income

Question 25a

Which category best represents your annual household income?

Results

- 54% had an income between $50,000 and $149,999 (see Figure 18).

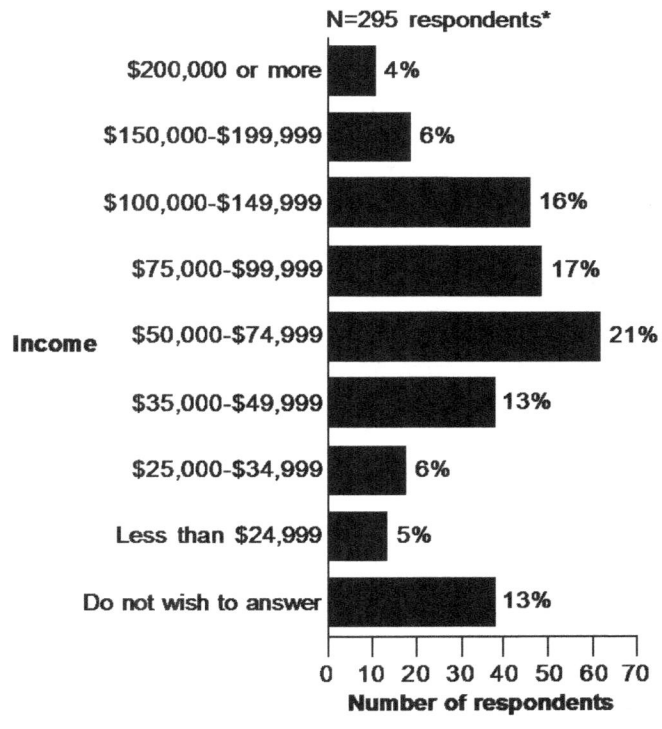

Figure 18. Respondent's level of income

Household size

Question 25b

How many people are in your household?

Results

- 58% of respondents had two people in their household (see Figure 19).

- 16% had one person.

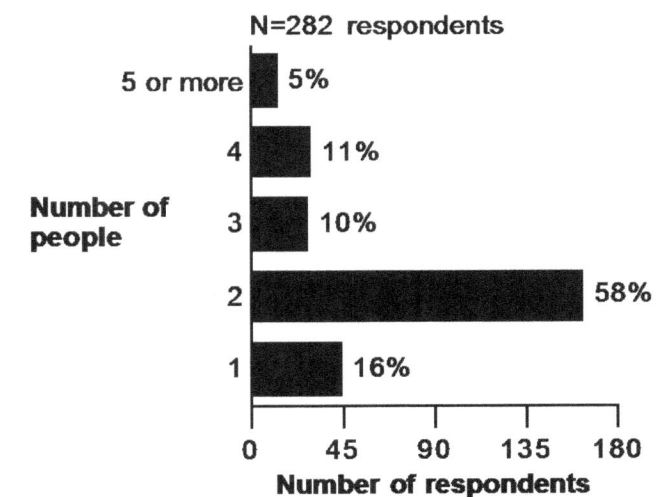

Figure 19. Number of people in household

*total percentages do not equal 100 due to rounding
**total percentages do not equal 100 because visitors could select more than one answer

Awareness of park programs

Question 2

Prior to your visit, were you and your personal group aware of programs (ranger-led walks, canoe trips, presentations, school group tours, etc.) offered in Congaree NP?

Results
- 59% of visitor groups were aware of programs offered at the park (see Figure 20).

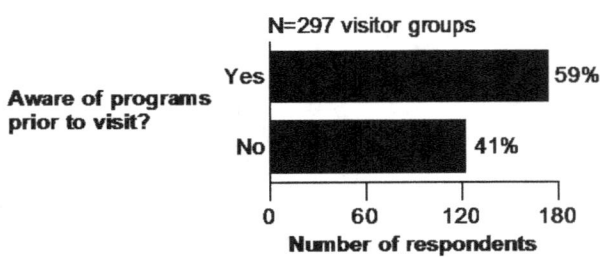

Figure 20. Visitor groups that were aware of programs in Congaree NP

Park name change and decision to visit

Question 3a

In 2003, Congaree Swamp National Monument became Congaree National Park. Did this name change have any effect on your decision to visit?

Results
- 15% of respondents said their decision to visit was affected by the name change (see Figure 21).

Question 3b

If YES, what effect did it have? (Open-ended)

- 48 respondents commented on the effect of the park's name change (see Table 9.)

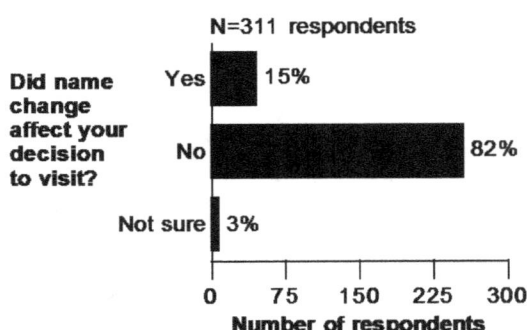

Figure 21. Visitor groups for whom the name change affected decision to visit

Table 9. Reasons for visiting due to new name (N=48 comments)

Comment	Number of times mentioned
Goal is to visit all parks/as many as possible	26
Raised awareness/motivated our visit	6
National park status is a draw	4
Added significance/elevated status	3
Made it more attractive to visit	3
It is a national park	2
Had great experiences with other national parks	1
National monument to national park	1
To me a monument is a statue or building	1
Wanted to support it even more	1

*total percentages do not equal 100 due to rounding
**total percentages do not equal 100 because visitors could select more than one answer

Knowledge of congressionally designated wilderness

Question 4a

Prior to your visit, were you aware of what congressionally designated wilderness is?

Results

- 57% of respondents were familiar with congressionally designated wilderness (see Figure 22).

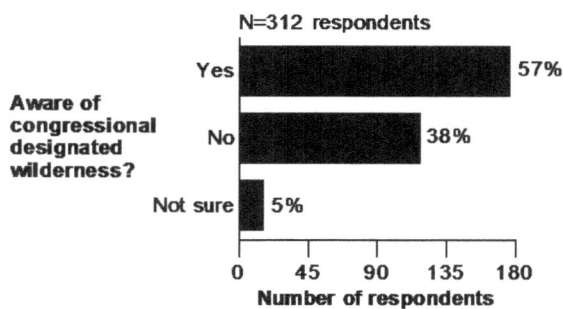

Figure 22. Respondents who were aware of what congressionally designated wilderness is

Question 4b

If NO, did you and your personal group learn about congressionally designated wilderness during your visit?

Results

- 46% of visitor groups said they learned about wilderness at Congaree NP during their visit (see Figure 23).

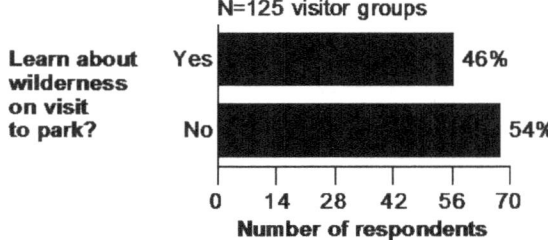

Figure 23. Visitor groups that learned about congressionally designated wilderness at park

Park policy to remove non-native species

Question 5

The National Park Service has a policy to control or remove non-native plants and animals from within park boundaries. Non-native species occupy an area that is not part of their natural, historic range, and often originated from another continent or region. Many of these species are invasive and damage park resources. Were you aware of this policy prior to your visit to Congaree NP?

Results

- 42% of respondents were aware of the policy to remove non-native species (see Figure 24).

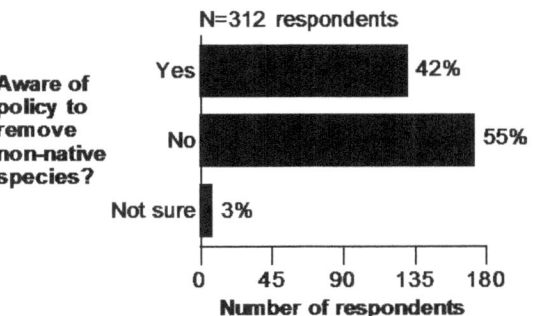

Figure 24. Respondents aware of park policy regarding non-native species

---

*total percentages do not equal 100 due to rounding
**total percentages do not equal 100 because visitors could select more than one answer

Support for policy to remove non-native species

Question 6

Would you and your personal group be supportive of the control and removal of non-native species at Congaree NP?

Results

- 83% of visitor groups were supportive of the removal non-native plants (see Figure 25).

- 73% were supportive of the removal of non-native animals (see Figure 26).

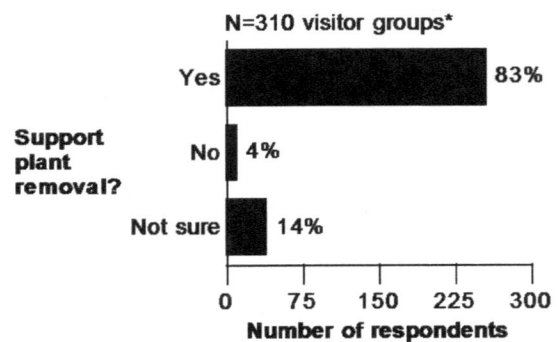

Figure 25. Visitor groups supporting the removal of non-native plants

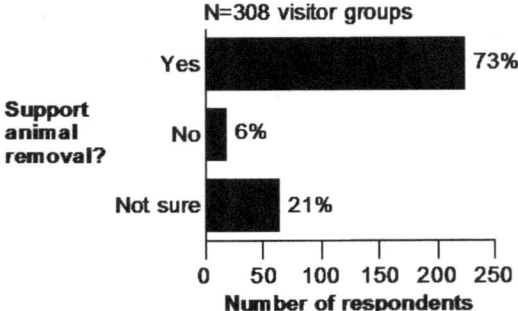

Figure 26. Visitor groups supporting the removal of non-native animals

---

*total percentages do not equal 100 due to rounding
**total percentages do not equal 100 because visitors could select more than one answer

Awareness of research and education in the park

Question 15a

Prior to this visit, were you and your personal group aware that Congaree NP is the home to the Old-Growth Bottomland Forest Research and Education Center, one of 21 centers nationwide?

Results

- 23% of visitor groups were aware of the Research and Education Center before visit (see Figure 27).

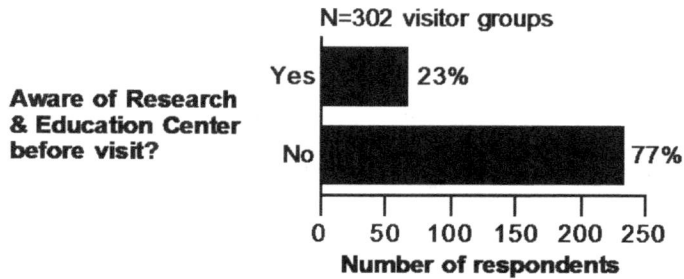

Figure 27. Visitor groups aware of Research and Education Center before visit

Question 15b

Did you and your personal group notice any scientists, scientific markers, or scientific equipment at work while you were in the park?

Results

- 40% of visitor groups noticed scientists, scientific markers, or scientific equipment at work in the park (see Figure 28).

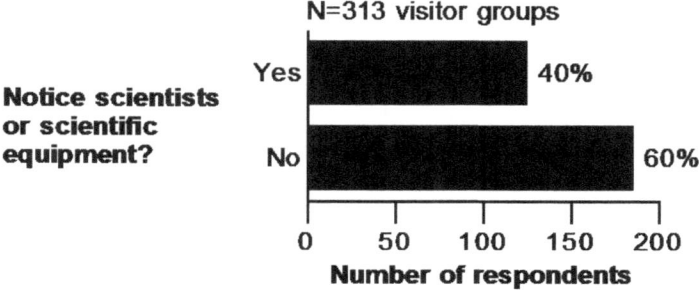

Figure 28. Visitor groups who noticed scientists, scientific markers, or scientific equipment at work during this visit

Question 15c

Did you and your personal group – through programs and products – learn about actual results of scientific studies in the park?

Results

- 25% of visitor groups learned about research results through programs and products while in the park (see Figure 29).

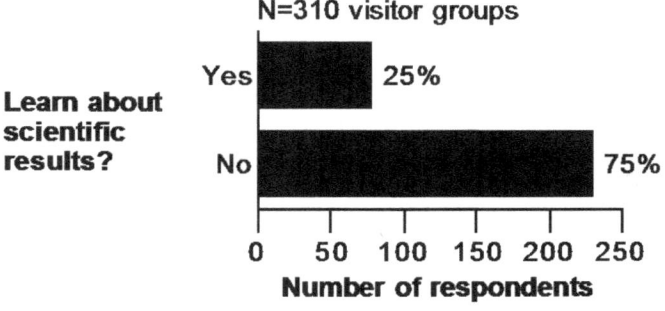

Figure 29. Visitor groups who learned about current scientific results in the park

*total percentages do not equal 100 due to rounding
**total percentages do not equal 100 because visitors could select more than one answer

Trip/Visit Characteristics and Preferences

Information sources prior to visit

Question 1
Prior to your visit, how did you and your personal group obtain information about Congaree NP?

Results
- 91% of visitor groups obtained information about Congaree NP prior to their visit (see Figure 30).

- As shown in Figure 31, among those visitor groups that obtained information about Congaree NP prior to their visit, the most common sources were:

  50% Park website
  30% Friends/relatives or
      word of mouth
  22% Previous visits

- "Other" sources (5%) were:

  Air National Guard that
      constructed roof
  Book on SC gardens
  Columbia Parks
  Life goal to visit all NPs
  National Park passport book
  New English Hiking Holidays
  Richland recreation trip
  Santee Birding Festival
  State Fair
  Teacher Ranger program

- Other websites used (5%) were:

  Google.com
  Backpack.com
  Terragaleria.com
  USA.rese.de
  Carolina Tourism board
  Columbia Visitor's website
  Georgia Tourism board
  National Park Traveler

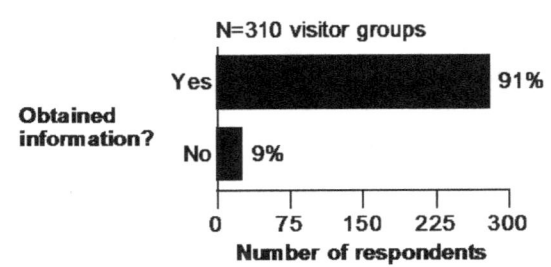

Figure 30. Visitor groups that obtained information prior to visit

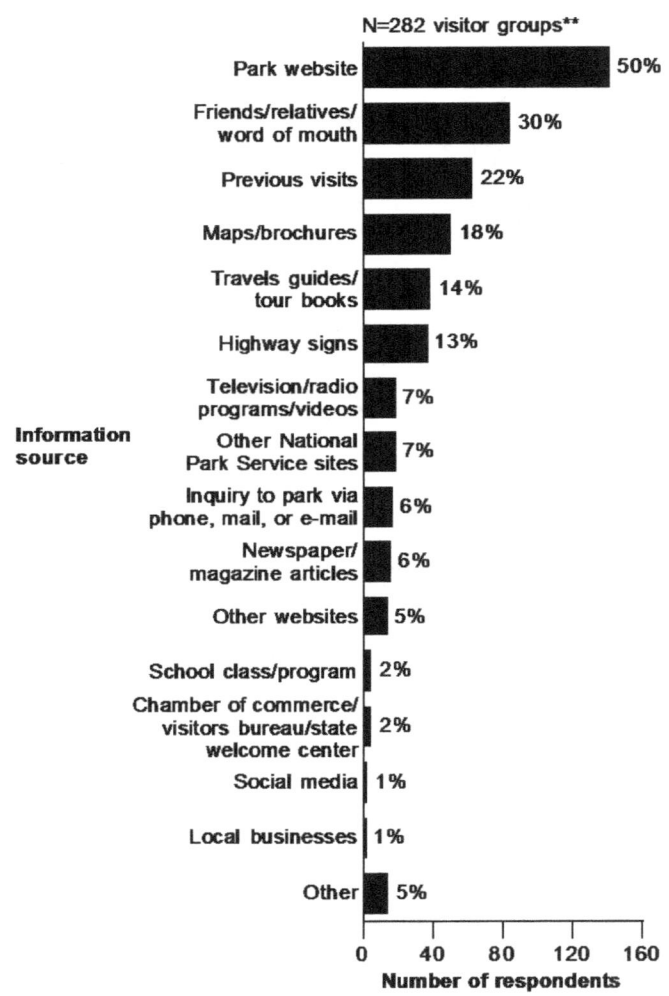

Figure 31. Sources of information

---

*total percentages do not equal 100 due to rounding
**total percentages do not equal 100 because visitors could select more than one answer

Park as destination

Question from on-site interview

A two-minute interview was conducted with each individual selected to complete the questionnaire. During the interview, the question was asked: "How did this visit to Congaree NP fit into your personal group's travel plans?"

Results

- 74% of visitor groups indicated that the park was their primary destination (see Figure 32).

- 21% said the visit to Congaree NP was one of several destinations.

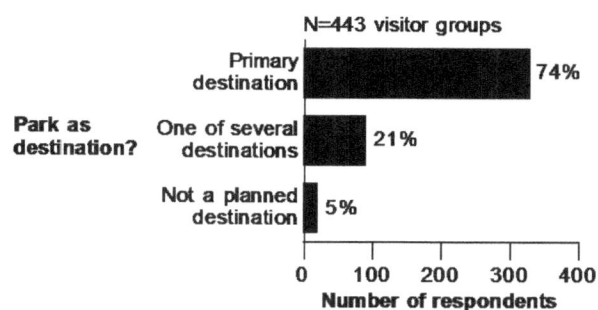

Figure 32. How visit to park fit into visitor groups' travel plans

---

*total percentages do not equal 100 due to rounding
**total percentages do not equal 100 because visitors could select more than one answer

Alternate recreation site

Question 24a

On this trip, if you and your personal group had not chosen to visit Congaree NP, what other recreation site would you have visited instead? (Open-ended)

Results

- 58% of visitor groups (N=180) responded to this question.

- Table 10 lists the places that visitor groups indicated as potential alternative sites they would have visited instead of Congaree NP.

Table 10. Alternate recreation sites (N=180 comments)

Site	Number of times mentioned
None	43
Riverbanks Zoo	19
Another state/national park/forest	11
Don't know	9
Multiple sites listed	9
Unspecified location	8
Sesquicentennial State Park	6
Francis Beidler Audubon Forest	5
Harbison State Forest	5
Columbia Riverwalk	4
Great Smoky Mountains National Park	4
Lake Murray	4
Myrtle Beach	4
Riverfront Park	4
Poinsett State Park	3
Santee NWR	3
Beach	2
Charleston, SC	2
Ft Jackson	2
Other locations	33

Question 24b

How far is this alternative site from your home?

Results
- 56% of the visitor groups indicated that they would travel up to 50 miles from their home to visit the alternate site (see Figure 33).

- 27% travel would more than 201 miles.

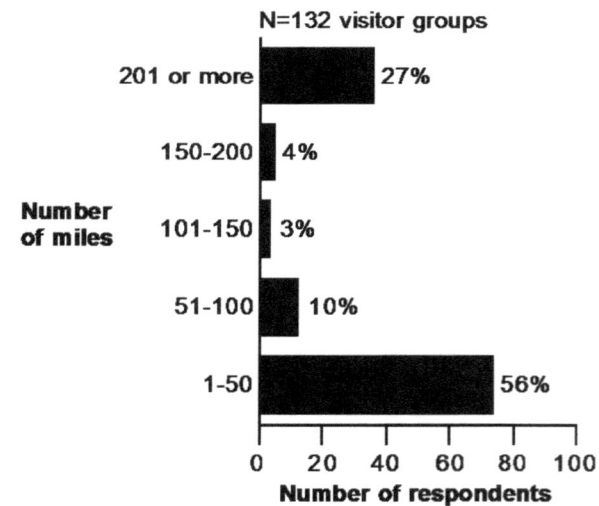

Figure 33. Number of miles to alternate recreation sites

---

*total percentages do not equal 100 due to rounding

**total percentages do not equal 100 because visitors could select more than one answer

Primary reason for visiting the park

Question 7
On this trip, what was the primary reason that you and your personal group came to the Congaree NP area (within 1-hour drive of the park)?

Results
- 29% of visitor groups were residents of the area (see Figure 34).

- As shown in Figure 35, the primary reason for visiting the area (within 1-hour drive of the park) among non-resident visitor groups were:

  65% Visit the park
  12% Visit friends/ relatives in the area

- "Other" primary reasons (3%) were:

  Brought four elementary students to observe filming crew
  Fort Jackson graduation service
  Get exercise
  Junior Ranger Camp Program registration
  Military trip in the area
  RV overnight parking
  USC graduation
  Vacation

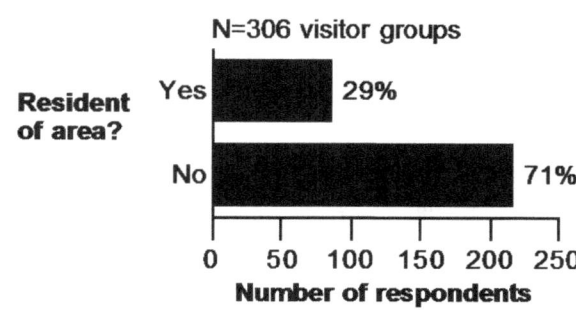

Figure 34. *Residents of the area (within 1-hour drive of the park)*

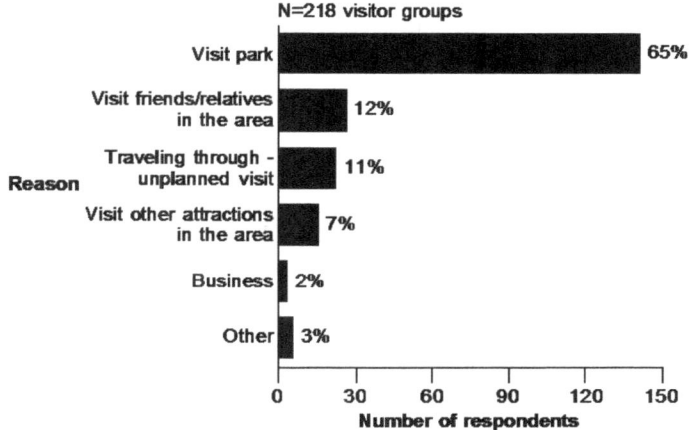

Figure 35. *Primary reason for visiting the park area (within 1-hour drive of the park)*

_____
*total percentages do not equal 100 due to rounding
**total percentages do not equal 100 because visitors could select more than one answer

Number of vehicles

Question 12
   On this visit, how many vehicles did you and your personal group use to arrive at the park?

Results
   • 93% of visitor groups used one vehicle to arrive at the park (see Figure 36).

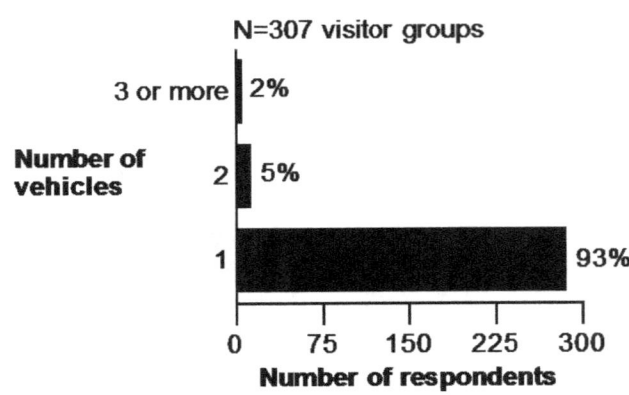

N=307 visitor groups

Figure 36. Number of vehicles used to arrive at the park

Overnight stays

Question 9a
   On this trip, did you and your personal group stay overnight away from your permanent residence either inside Congaree NP or within the nearby area (within 1-hour drive of the park)?

Results
   • 40% of visitor groups stayed overnight away from home either in the park or the area (see Figure 37).

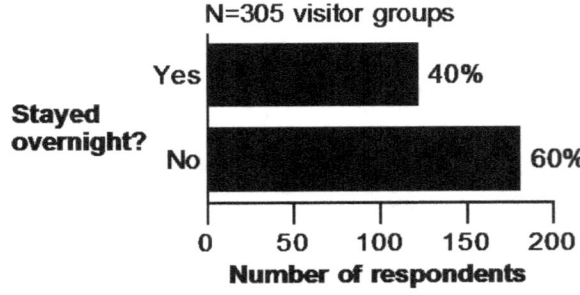

N=305 visitor groups

Figure 37. Visitor groups that stayed overnight in the park or within 1-hour drive of the park

Question 9b
   If YES, how many nights did you and your personal group spend inside the park.

Results – Interpret with **CAUTION!**

   • Not enough visitor groups responded to provide reliable results (see Figure 38).

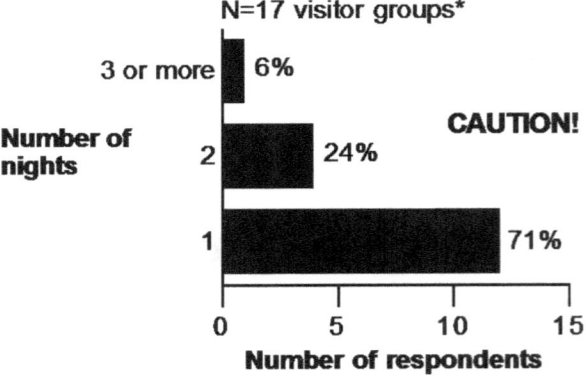

N=17 visitor groups*

Figure 38. Number of nights spent inside the park

---

*total percentages do not equal 100 due to rounding
**total percentages do not equal 100 because visitors could select more than one answer

Question 9c
If YES, how many nights did you and your personal group spend outside the park within 1-hour drive?

Results
- 49% of visitor groups stayed one night outside the park within 1-hour drive of the park (see Figure 39).

- 34% stayed two or three nights.

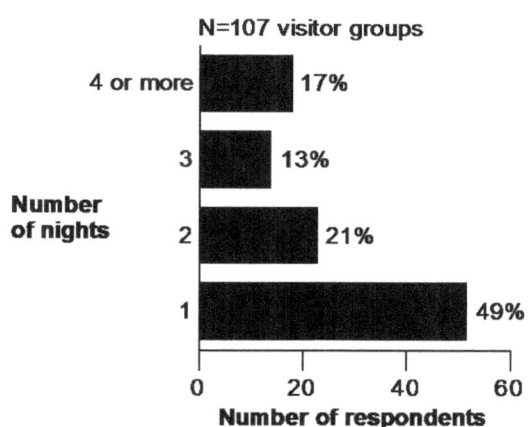

Figure 39. Number of nights spent in the area outside the park (within 1-hour drive of the park).

Accommodations used inside the park

Question 9b
In which types of accommodations did you and your personal group spend the night(s) inside the park?

Results
- Interpret with **CAUTION!** Not enough visitor groups stayed overnight in the park to provide reliable results (see Figure 40)

- Table 11 shows the number of nights spent in accommodations inside the park.

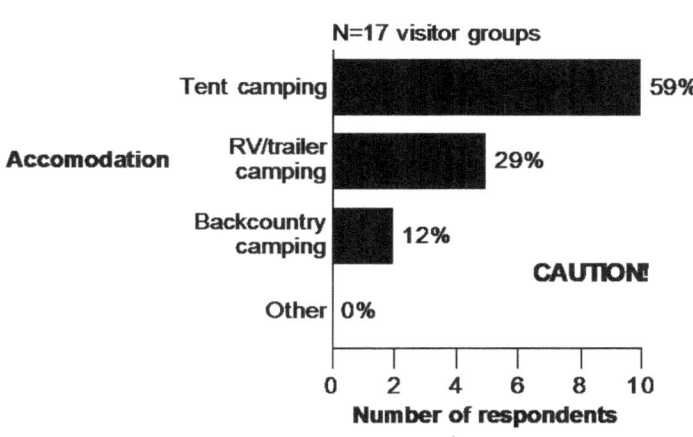

Figure 40. Accommodations used inside the park

Table 11. Number of nights spent in accommodations inside the park - **CAUTION!** (N=number of visitor groups that specified the number of nights in each type of accommodation)

Accommodation	N	Number of nights (%)			
		1	2	3	4 or more
RV/trailer camping	5	80	20	0	0
Tent camping	10	70	20	10	0
Backcountry camping	2	50	50	0	0
Other	0	0	0	0	0

*total percentages do not equal 100 due to rounding
**total percentages do not equal 100 because visitors could select more than one answer

Accommodations used outside the park

Question 9c

In which types of accommodations did you and your personal group spend the night(s) outside park within 1-hour drive?

Results

- 83% of visitor groups stayed overnight, in a lodge, hotel, motel, rented condo/home, or bed & breakfast (see Figure 41).

- Table 12 shows the number of nights spent at accommodations outside the park within 1-hour drive of the park.

- "Other" accommodations (1%) were not specified.

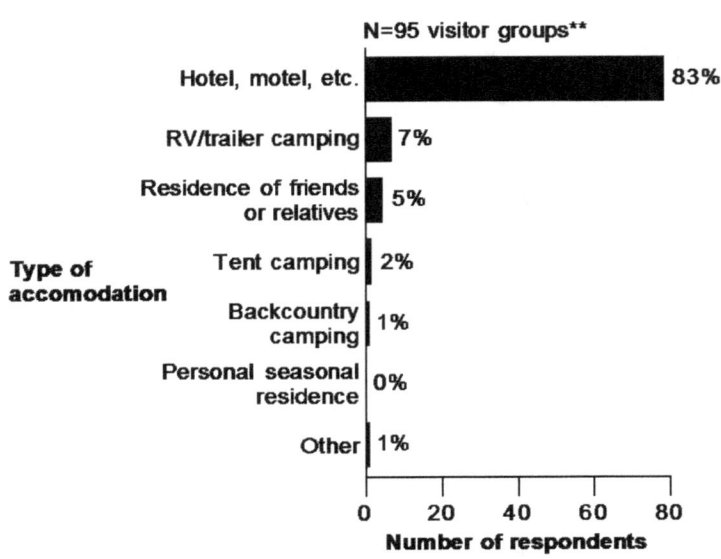

Figure 41. Accommodations used outside the park within 1-hour drive

Table 12. Number of nights spent at accommodations outside the park within 1-hour drive (N=number of visitor groups that specified the number of nights spent in each type of accommodation)

Type of accommodation	N	Number of nights (%) *			
		1	2	3	4 or more
Lodge, hotel, motel, cabin, rented condo/home, or bed & breakfast	79	53	22	13	13
RV/trailer camping – **CAUTION!**	7	29	14	14	43
Tent camping – **CAUTION!**	2	50	50	0	0
Backcountry camping – **CAUTION!**	1	100	0	0	0
Personal seasonal residence – **CAUTION!**	0	0	0	0	0
Residence of friends or relatives – **CAUTION!**	15	33	27	20	20
Other accommodations – **CAUTION!**	3	33	0	0	67

*total percentages do not equal 100 due to rounding
**total percentages do not equal 100 because visitors could select more than one answer

Length of stay in the park

Question 13b
On this visit, how long did you and your personal group spend visiting Congaree NP?

Results

Number of hours if less than 24

- 50% spent three to four hours in the park (see Figure 42).

- 36% of visitor groups spent one to two hours.

- The average length of stay for visitor groups who spent less than 24 hours was 3.2 hours.

Number of days if 24 hours or more

- Interpret with **CAUTION!** Not enough visitor groups responded to provide reliable results (see Figure 43).

- The average length of stay in the park for all visitor groups was 6.1 hours

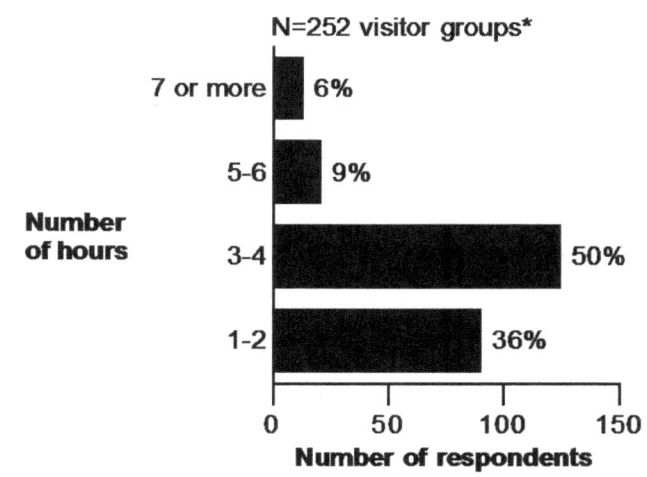

Figure 42. Number of hours spent in the park

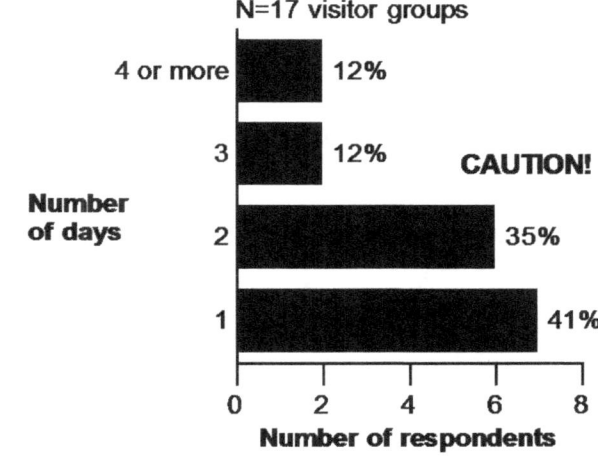

Figure 43. Number of days spent in the park

*total percentages do not equal 100 due to rounding
**total percentages do not equal 100 because visitors could select more than one answer

Length of stay in the park area

Question 13a

How long did you and your personal group stay in the Congaree NP area (within 1-hour drive of the park)?

Results

- 33% of visitor groups were residents of the area within 1-hour drive of the park (see Figure 44).

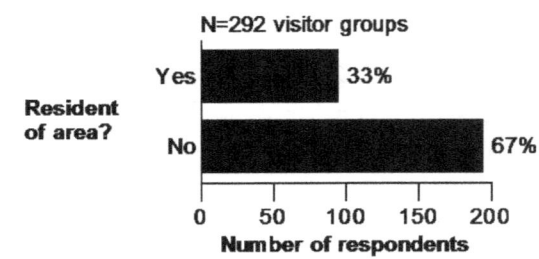

Figure 44. Residents of the area (within a1-hour drive of the park)

Number of hours if less than 24

- 39% of visitor groups spent one to two hours in the park area (see Figure 45).

- 36% spent three to four hours.

- 14% spent seven or more hours.

- The average length of stay in the area for visitor groups who spent less than 24 hours was 4.1 hours.

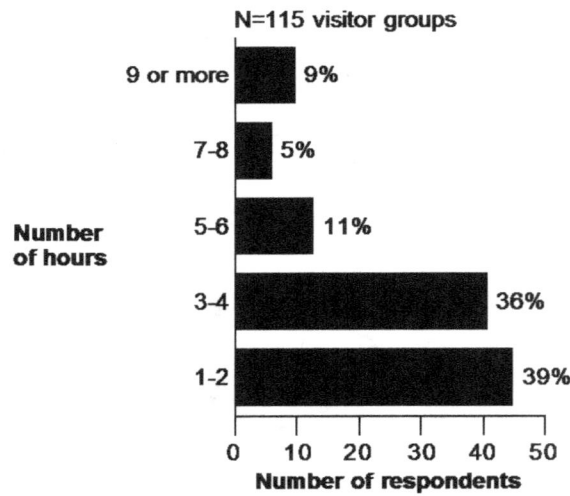

Figure 45. Number of hours spent in the park area

Number of days if 24 hours or more

- 59% of visitor groups spent one to two days in the park area (see Figure 46).

- 25% spent three to four days.

- 16% spent five or more days.

- The average length of stay for visitor groups that spent 24 hours or more was 3.6 days.

- The average length of stay for all visitor groups was 38.1 hours, or 1.6 days.

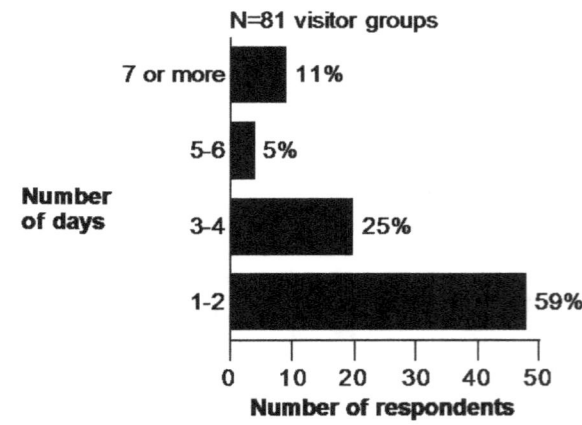

Figure 46. Number of days spent in the park area

---

*total percentages do not equal 100 due to rounding
**total percentages do not equal 100 because visitors could select more than one answer

Sites visited in the Congaree NP area

Question 8
On this visit, which sites did you and your personal group visit in the Congaree NP area (within 1-hour drive of the park)?

- As shown in Figure 47, the sites most commonly visited in the Congaree NP area were:

    26% South Carolina state parks
    25% University of South Carolina
    22% State Capitol

- The least visited site was:

    1% National Advocacy Center

- "Other" sites (20%) visited are shown in Table 13.

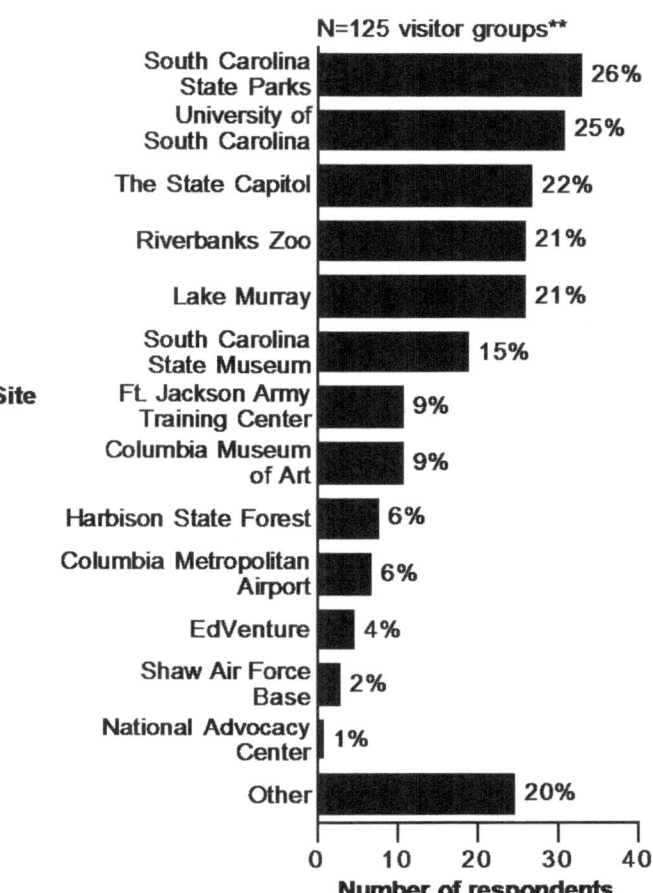

Figure 47. Sites visited in the park area

---

*total percentages do not equal 100 due to rounding
**total percentages do not equal 100 because visitors could select more than one answer

Table 13. "Other" sites visited in the park area

Site	Number of Respondents
Congaree River	2
Darlington Raceway	2
Swan Lake and Gardens	2
Blue Ridge Mountains	1
Broad River	1
Cayce Park	1
Charleston	1
Charleston Orangeburg Rose Festival	1
Darlington	1
Eastover	1
Fort Sumter	1
Francis Beidler Audubon Forest	1
G-Mart	1
Harbison Mall	1
Kohl's department store	1
Lexington County Museum	1
National battlefields	1
Orangeburg Edisto Memorial Park	1
Poinsett State Park	1
Riverwalk	1
Saluda River	1
Santee	1
State farmers market	1
Sumter	1
Woodgone Woodworking Store	1

*total percentages do not equal 100 due to rounding
**total percentages do not equal 100 because visitors could select more than one answer

Activities within the park

Question 11

On this visit, in which activities did you and your personal group participate within Congaree NP?

Results

- As shown in Figure 48, The most common activities which visitor groups participated in were:

  82% Walking/hiking
  71% Visiting the visitor center
  24% Birdwatching

- "Other" activities (3%) were:

  Photography
  Obtaining NP passport stamp

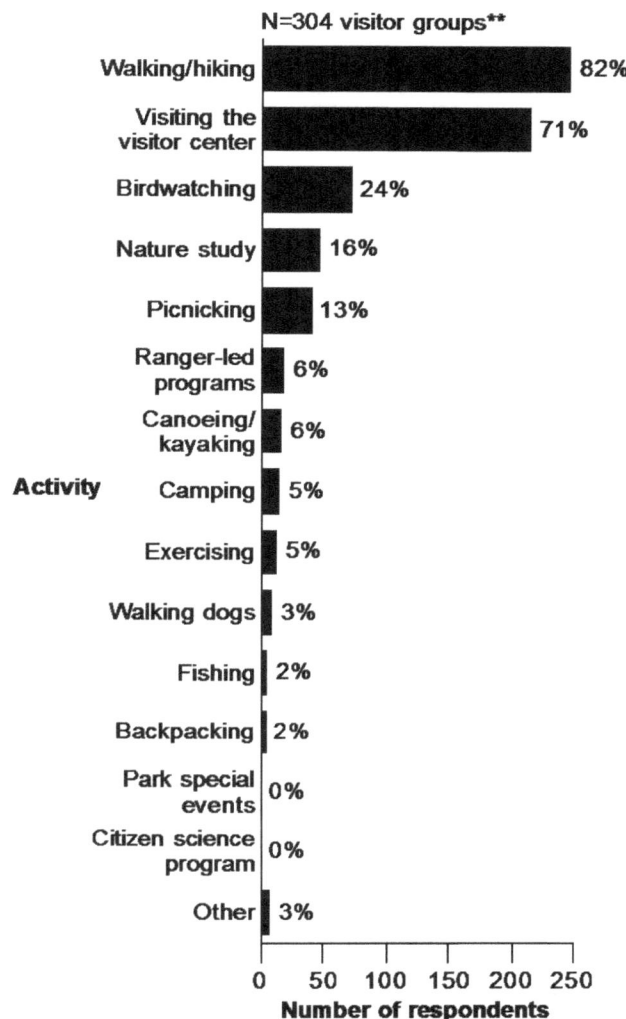

Figure 48. Activities on this visit

*total percentages do not equal 100 due to rounding
**total percentages do not equal 100 because visitors could select more than one answer

Use of park trails

Question 10a

On this visit to Congaree NP, did you and your personal group walk/canoe/kayak any park trails?

Results

- 92% of visitor groups used a trail in Congaree NP (see Figure 49).

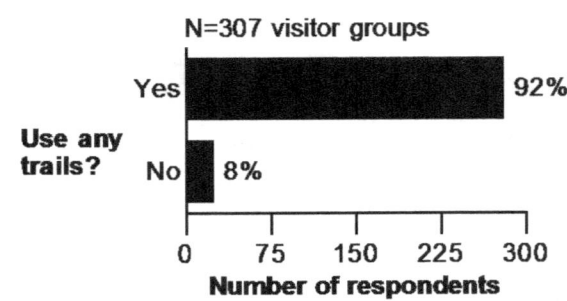

Figure 49. Visitor groups that used park trails

Question 10b

If YES, which of the following trails did you and your personal group walk/canoe/kayak on this visit?

Results

- As shown in Figure 50, of those visitor groups that used park trails, the most commonly used trails were:

    81% Elevated Boardwalk Trail
    62% Low Boardwalk Trail
    30% Weston Lake Loop Trail

- The least used trail was the Kingsnake Trail (2%).

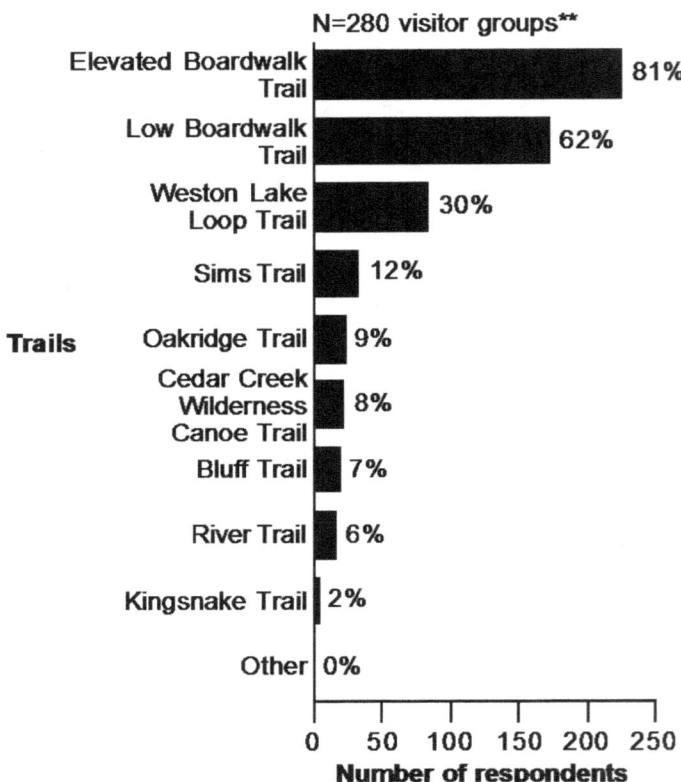

Figure 50. Trails used in Congaree NP

---

*total percentages do not equal 100 due to rounding
**total percentages do not equal 100 because visitors could select more than one answer

Ratings of Services, Facilities, Attributes, Resources and Elements

Information services and facilities used

Question 16a
Please indicate all of the information services and facilities that you or your personal group used at Congaree NP during this visit.

Results
- As shown in Figure 51, the most common information services and facilities used by visitor groups were:

  86% Park brochure/ map
  78% Assistance from park staff
  74% Visitor center exhibits

- The least used service/ facility was Junior Ranger programs (3%).

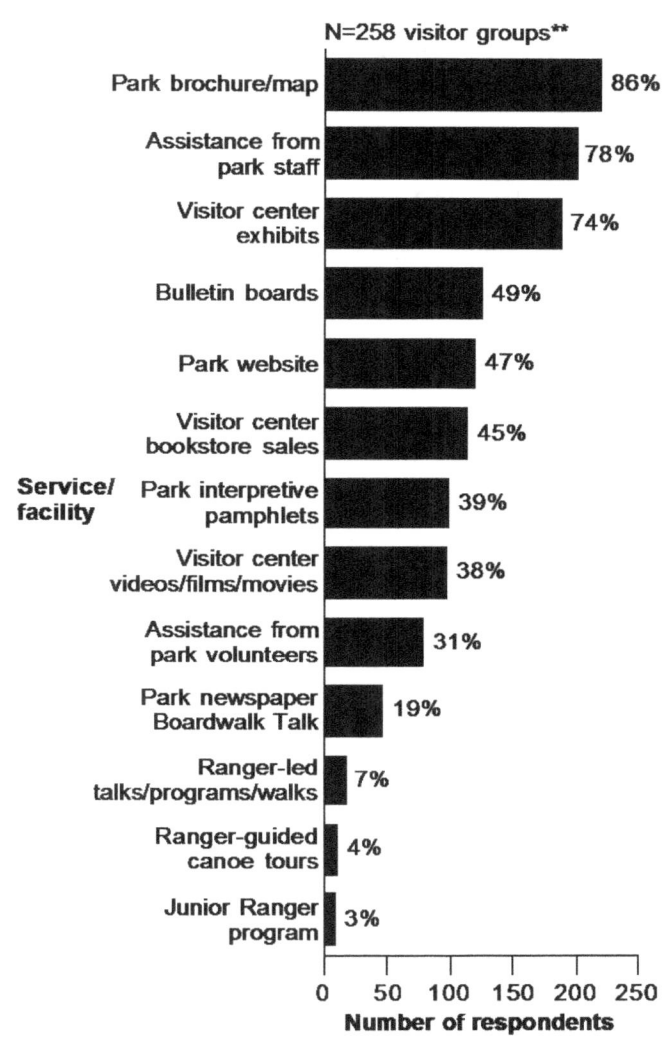

Figure 51. Information services and facilities used

---

*total percentages do not equal 100 due to rounding
**total percentages do not equal 100 because visitors could select more than one answer

Importance ratings of information services and facilities

Question 16b
For only those services and facilities that you or your personal group used, please rate their importance to your visit from 1-5.

    1=Not important
    2=Somewhat important
    3=Moderately important
    4=Very important
    5=Extremely important

Results
- Figure 52 shows the combined proportions of "extremely important" and "very important" ratings of information services and facilities that were rated by 30 or more visitor groups.

- The services and facilities receiving the highest combined proportions of "extremely important" and "very important" ratings were:

    90% Park brochure/map
    89% Park interpretive pamphlets
    86% Park website

- Table 14 shows the importance ratings of each service and facility.

- The service/facility receiving the highest "not important" rating that was rated by 30 or more visitor groups was:

    3% Assistance from park volunteers

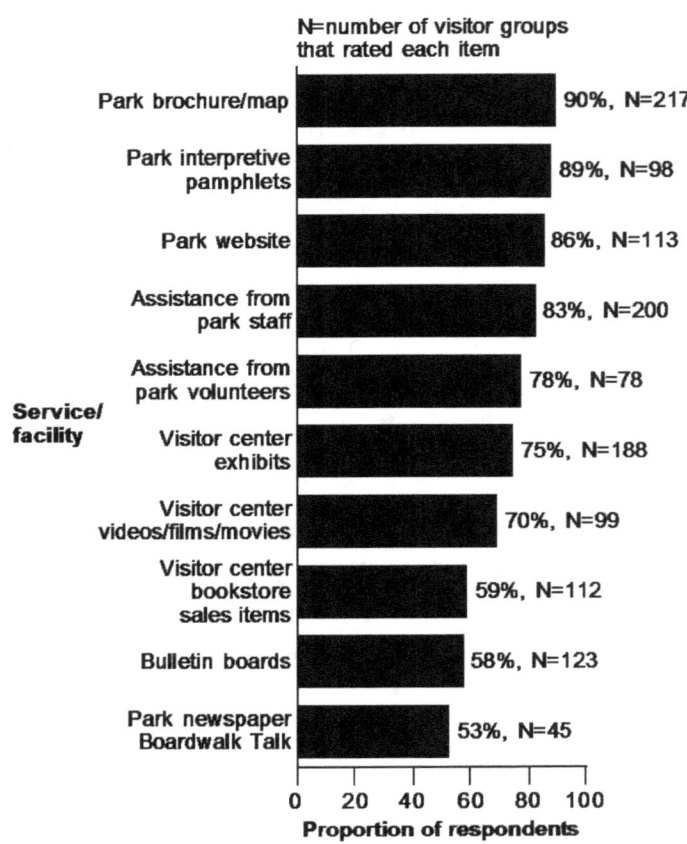

Figure 52. Combined proportions of "extremely important" and "very important" ratings of information services and facilities

---

*total percentages do not equal 100 due to rounding
**total percentages do not equal 100 because visitors could select more than one answer

Table 14. Importance ratings of information services and facilities
(N=number of visitor groups that rated each service and facility)

Service/facility	N	Rating (%)*				
		Not important	Somewhat important	Moderately important	Very important	Extremely important
Assistance from park staff	200	1	3	14	39	44
Assistance from park volunteers	78	3	5	14	45	33
Bulletin boards	123	1	7	34	33	25
Junior Ranger program - **CAUTION!**	9	11	0	33	22	33
Park brochure/map	217	0	2	8	35	55
Park interpretive pamphlets	98	0	1	10	37	52
Park newspaper *Boardwalk Talk*	45	0	13	33	29	24
Park website (nps.gov/cong)	113	0	3	12	31	55
Ranger-led talks/ programs/walks - **CAUTION!**	18	0	0	17	39	44
Ranger-guided canoe tours - **CAUTION!**	11	0	0	0	46	55
Visitor center bookstore sales items	112	1	10	30	37	22
Visitor center videos/films/movies	99	0	5	24	46	24
Visitor center exhibits	188	1	2	22	43	31

*total percentages do not equal 100 due to rounding
**total percentages do not equal 100 because visitors could select more than one answer

Quality ratings of information services and facilities

Question 16c

For only those services and facilities that you or your personal group used, please rate their quality from 1-5.

        1=Very poor
        2=Poor
        3=Average
        4=Good
        5=Very good

Results

- Figure 53 shows the combined proportions of "very good" and "good" ratings of information services and facilities that were rated by 30 or more visitor groups.

- The services and facilities receiving the highest combined proportions of "very good" and "good" ratings were:

    98% Assistance from park volunteers
    95% Assistance from park staff
    91% Visitor center exhibits
    85% Park brochure/map

- Table 15 shows the quality ratings of each service and facility.

- The services/facilities receiving the highest "very poor" rating that was rated by 30 or more visitor groups were:

    1% Park brochure/map
    1% Visitor center bookstore sales items

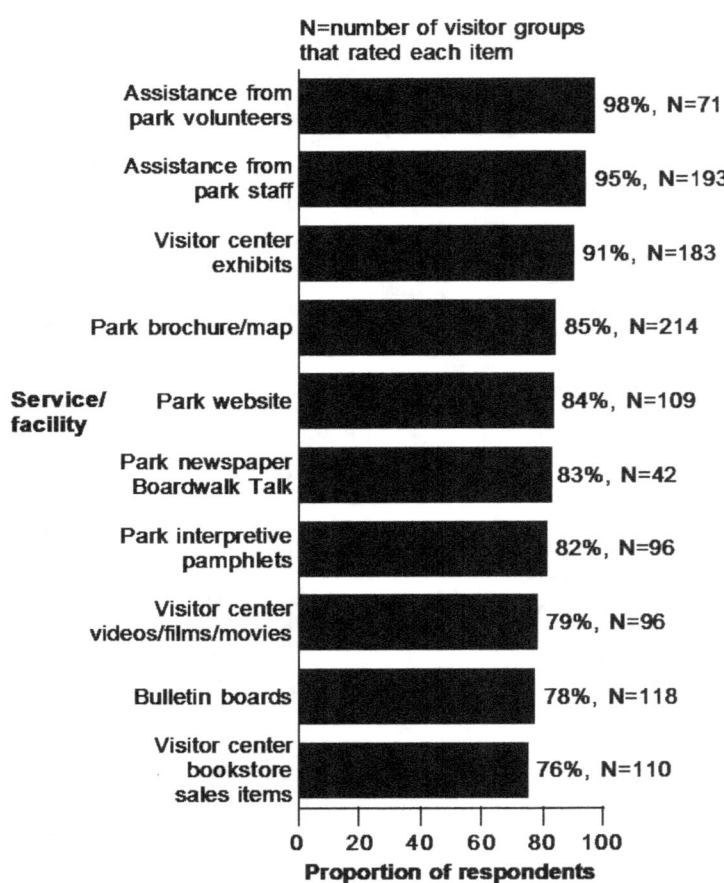

Figure 53. Combined proportions of "very good" and "good" ratings of information services and facilities

*total percentages do not equal 100 due to rounding
**total percentages do not equal 100 because visitors could select more than one answer

Table 15. Quality ratings of information services and facilities
(N=number of visitor groups that rated each service and facility)

Service/facility	N	Rating (%)*				
		Very poor	Poor	Average	Good	Very good
Assistance from park staff	193	0	1	4	18	77
Assistance from park volunteers	71	0	1	0	15	83
Bulletin boards	118	0	1	21	42	36
Junior Ranger program - **CAUTION!**	7	0	0	0	43	57
Park brochure/map	214	1	3	11	37	48
Park interpretive pamphlets	96	0	1	17	36	46
Park newspaper *Boardwalk Talk*	42	0	0	17	40	43
Park website (nps.gov/cong)	109	0	1	15	45	39
Ranger-led talks/ programs/walks - **CAUTION!**	15	0	0	7	33	60
Ranger-guided canoe tours - **CAUTION!**	9	0	0	0	33	67
Visitor center bookstore sales items	110	1	1	22	38	38
Visitor center videos/films/movies	96	0	4	17	32	47
Visitor center exhibits	183	0	1	9	37	54

*total percentages do not equal 100 due to rounding
**total percentages do not equal 100 because visitors could select more than one answer

Mean scores of importance and quality ratings of information services and facilities

- Figures 54 and 55 show the mean scores of importance and quality ratings of information and facilities that were rated by 30 or more visitor groups.

- All information services and facilities were rated above average.

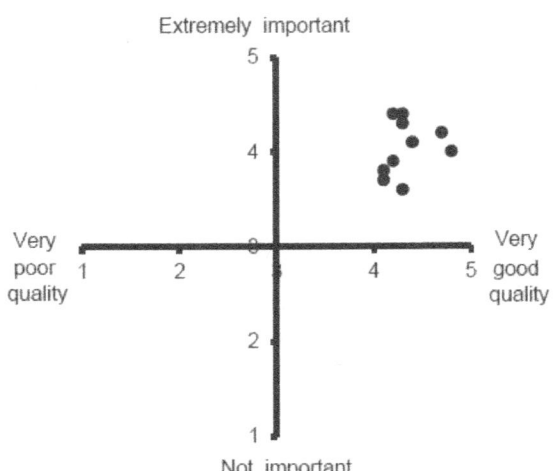

Figure 54. Mean scores of importance and quality ratings of information services and facilities

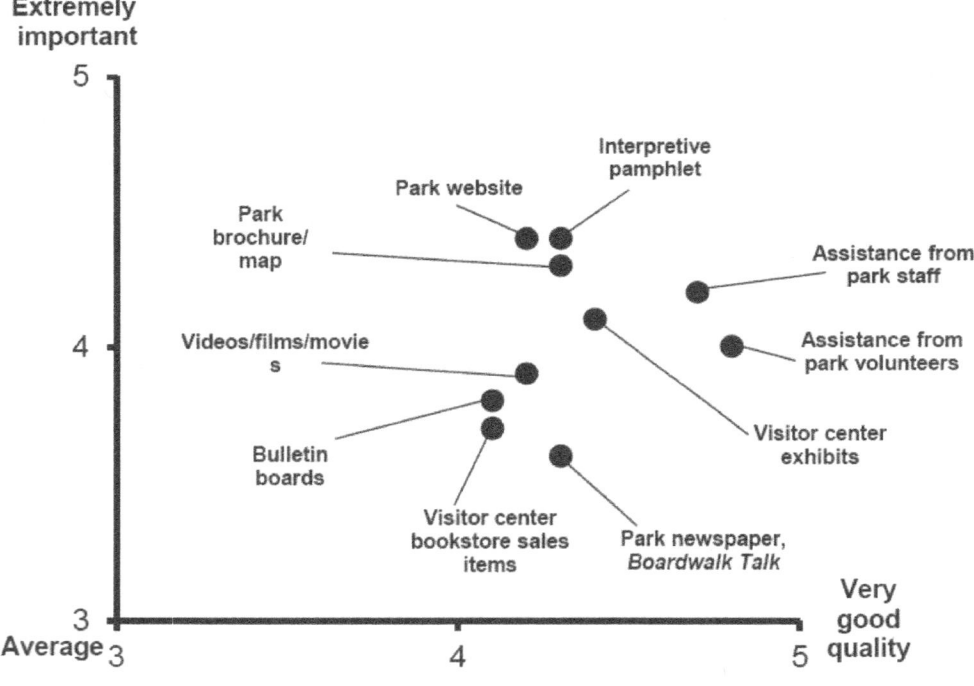

Figure 55. Detail of Figure 54

---

*total percentages do not equal 100 due to rounding

**total percentages do not equal 100 because visitors could select more than one answer

Visitor services and facilities used

Question 17a
Please indicate all of the visitor services and facilities that you or your personal group used at Congaree NP during this visit.

Results
- As shown in Figure 56, the most common visitor services and facilities used by visitor groups were:

  89% Boardwalks
  86% Restrooms
  83% Parking areas

- The least used service/facility was:

  2% Backcountry camping

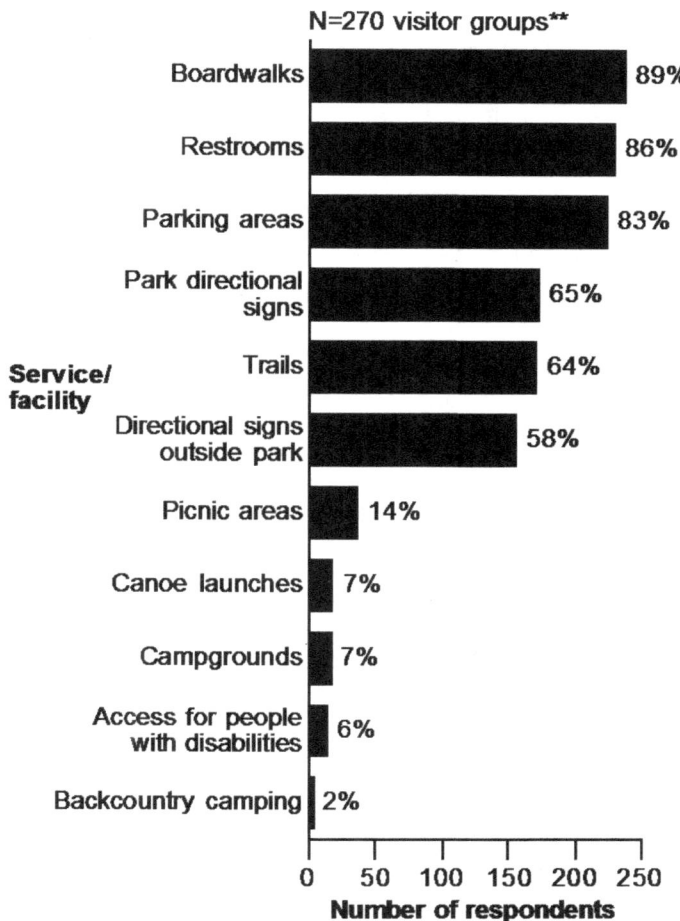

Figure 56. Visitor services and facilities used

---

*total percentages do not equal 100 due to rounding
**total percentages do not equal 100 because visitors could select more than one answer

Importance ratings of visitor services and facilities

Question 17b
  For only those services and facilities that you or your personal group used, please rate their importance to your visit from 1-5.

       1=Not important
       2=Somewhat important
       3=Moderately important
       4=Very important
       5=Extremely important

Results
  • Figure 57 shows the combined proportions of "extremely important" and "very important" ratings of visitor services and facilities that were rated by 30 or more visitor groups.

  • The visitor services and facilities receiving the highest combined proportions of "extremely important" and "very important" ratings were:

       98% Trails
       94% Park directional signs
       89% Restrooms
       88% Directional signs outside the park

  • Table 16 shows the importance ratings of each service and facility.

  • The service/facility receiving the highest "not important" rating that was rated by 30 or more visitor groups was:

       2% Boardwalks

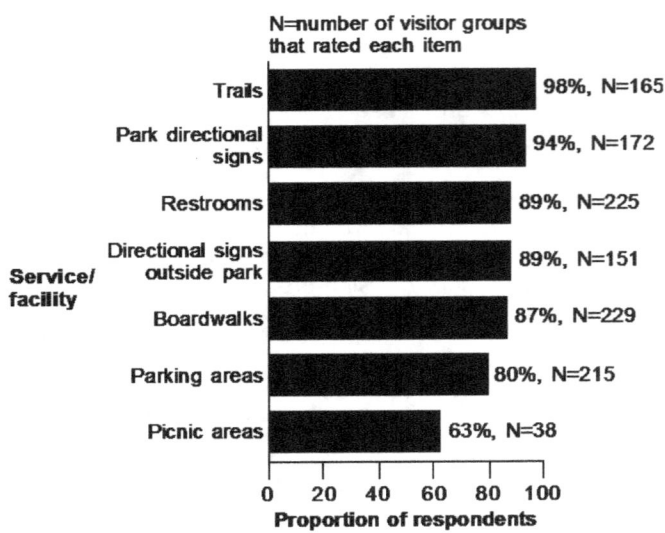

Figure 57. Combined proportions of "extremely important" and "very important" ratings of visitor services and facilities

---

*total percentages do not equal 100 due to rounding
**total percentages do not equal 100 because visitors could select more than one answer

Table 16. Importance ratings of visitor services and facilities
(N=number of visitor groups that rated each service and facility)

Service/facility	N	Rating (%)*				
		Not important	Somewhat important	Moderately important	Very important	Extremely important
Access for people with disabilities - **CAUTION!**	16	0	0	0	31	69
Backcountry camping - **CAUTION!**	5	0	0	0	0	100
Boardwalks	229	2	1	10	27	60
Campgrounds - **CAUTION!**	18	0	0	0	33	67
Canoe launches - **CAUTION!**	19	0	0	11	32	58
Directional signs outside of park	151	0	1	10	32	57
Park directional signs	172	0	1	5	34	60
Parking areas	215	1	4	16	34	46
Picnic areas	38	0	0	37	26	37
Restrooms	225	0	1	10	28	61
Trails	165	0	0	2	29	69

*total percentages do not equal 100 due to rounding
**total percentages do not equal 100 because visitors could select more than one answer

Quality ratings of visitor services and facilities

Question 17c

For only those services and facilities that you or your personal group used, please rate their quality from 1-5.

1=Very poor
2=Poor
3=Average
4=Good
5=Very good

Results

- Figure 58 shows the combined proportions of "very good" and "good" ratings of visitor services and facilities that were rated by 30 or more visitor groups.

- The services and facilities receiving the highest combined proportions of "very good" and "good" ratings were:

  98% Boardwalks
  95% Trails
  95% Restrooms

- Table 17 shows the quality ratings of each service and facility.

- The service/facility receiving the highest "very poor" rating that was rated by 30 or more visitor groups was:

  5% Directional signs outside park

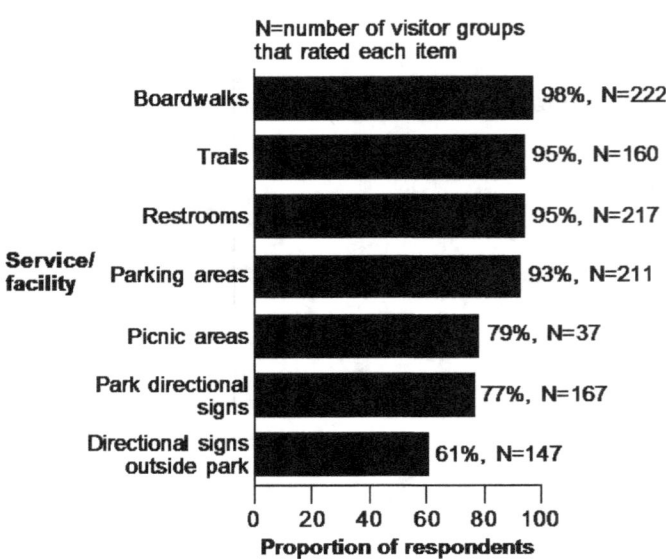

N=number of visitor groups that rated each item

Figure 58. Combined proportions of "very good" and "good" ratings of visitor services and facilities

---

*total percentages do not equal 100 due to rounding
**total percentages do not equal 100 because visitors could select more than one answer

Table 17. Quality ratings of visitor services and facilities
(N=number of visitor groups that rated each service and facility)

Service/facility	N	Rating (%)*				
		Very poor	Poor	Average	Good	Very good
Access for people with disabilities - **CAUTION!**	16	6	0	6	38	50
Backcountry camping - **CAUTION!**	5	0	0	40	20	40
Boardwalks	222	1	0	1	21	77
Campgrounds - **CAUTION!**	18	6	0	33	28	33
Canoe launches - **CAUTION!**	18	0	6	50	28	17
Directional signs outside of park	147	5	10	23	29	32
Park directional signs	167	3	2	17	35	42
Parking areas	211	1	0	6	34	59
Picnic areas	37	0	3	19	41	38
Restrooms	217	0	1	5	29	66
Trails	160	1	1	4	29	66

*total percentages do not equal 100 due to rounding
**total percentages do not equal 100 because visitors could select more than one answer

Mean scores of importance and quality ratings of visitor services and facilities

- Figures 59 and 60 show the mean scores of importance and quality ratings of visitor services and facilities that were rated by 30 or more visitor groups.

- All visitor services and facilities were rated above average.

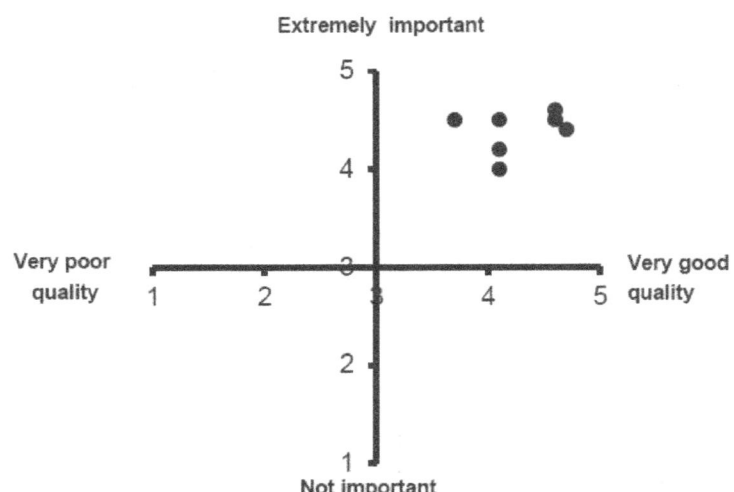

Figure 59. Mean scores of importance and quality of visitor services and facilities

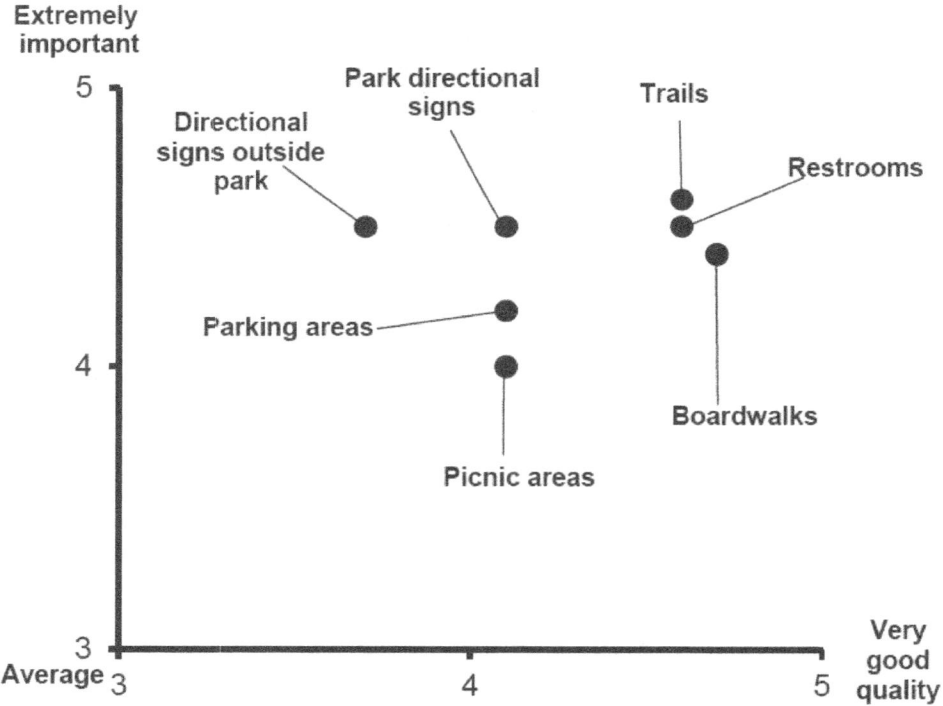

Figure 60. Detail of Figure 59

---

*total percentages do not equal 100 due to rounding
**total percentages do not equal 100 because visitors could select more than one answer

Importance of protecting park attributes, resources, and experiences

Question 14

It is the National Park Service's responsibility to protect Congaree NP natural, scenic, and cultural resources while at the same time providing for public enjoyment. How important is protection of the following resources/attributes in the park to you and your personal group?

1=Not important
2=Somewhat important
3=Moderately important
4=Very important
5=Extremely important

Results

- As shown in Figure 61, the highest combined proportions of "extremely important" and "very important" ratings of protecting park resources and attributes included:

  90% Native wildlife
  89% Natural quiet/ sounds of nature
  88% Clean water

- Table 18 shows the details of each resource/attribute and their ratings. The resource/attribute receiving the highest "not important" rating was:

  11% Clear night sky

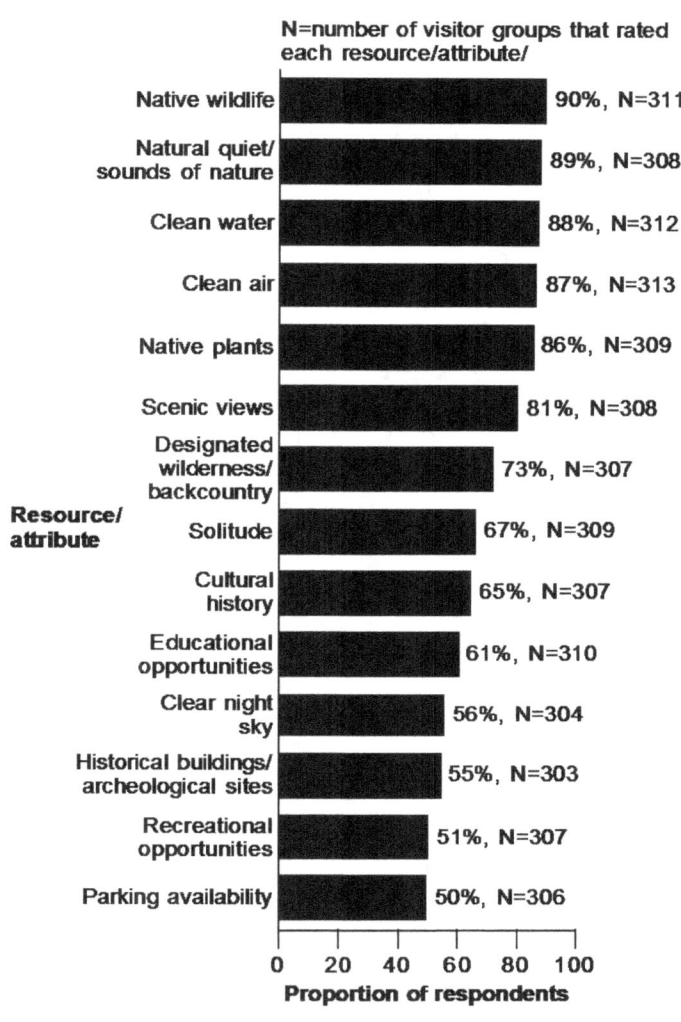

Figure 61. Combined proportions of "extremely important" and "very important" ratings of protecting park resources and attributes

---

*total percentages do not equal 100 due to rounding
**total percentages do not equal 100 because visitors could select more than one answer

Table 18. Visitor rating of importance of protecting park resources and attributes
(N=number of visitors that rated each resource/attribute)

Resource/attribute	N	Rating (%)*				
		Not important	Somewhat important	Moderately important	Very important	Extremely important
Clean air (visibility)	313	2	3	9	35	52
Clean water	312	2	2	9	31	57
Clear night sky (star gazing)	304	11	7	26	22	34
Cultural history (photographs/artifacts/oral histories)	307	4	9	22	37	28
Designated wilderness/backcountry	307	3	5	19	30	43
Educational opportunities	310	3	8	27	36	25
Historic buildings/archeological sites	303	6	12	27	29	26
Native plants	309	2	4	9	35	51
Native wildlife	311	1	3	5	34	56
Natural quiet/sounds of nature	308	1	2	8	27	62
Parking availability	306	3	14	33	33	17
Recreational opportunities	307	5	14	30	34	17
Scenic views	308	2	2	16	38	43
Solitude	309	3	4	27	29	38

*total percentages do not equal 100 due to rounding
**total percentages do not equal 100 because visitors could select more than one answer

Elements that affected park experience

Question 29

Please indicate how the following elements may have affected you and your personal group's park experience during this visit to Congaree NP?

Results

- Table 19 shows that the element that detracted from the greatest number of visitor groups was Airplane noise (12%).

- The element that added the most to visitor experiences was encountering small numbers of visitors on the trail (31%).

- Other elements that detracted from visitor experiences included:

  Mosquitoes (17 visitor groups)
  Noisy school children (4 visitor groups)
  People smoking on boardwalk (1 visitor group)
  Dog barking at campground (1 visitor group)

Table 19. Effects of different elements on the park experience
(N=number of visitors that rated each element)

Element	N	Rating (%)*			
		Detracted from	No effect	Added to	Did not experience
Airplane noise	297	12	26	1	62
Automobile noise	297	4	29	0	67
Gunshots from neighboring lands	297	2	16	0	82
Noise from park staff activities	298	1	21	0	78
Train noise	296	1	17	1	81
Other visitors' activities	297	10	58	4	29
Small number of visitors on trails	295	0	54	31	15
Large number of visitors on trails	290	8	24	2	66
Small number of visitors canoeing/kayaking	289	0	17	5	79
Large number of visitors canoeing/kayaking	289	1	15	1	84
Impact of wild pigs	296	7	14	10	69
Other	109	23	10	8	59

*total percentages do not equal 100 due to rounding
**total percentages do not equal 100 because visitors could select more than one answer

Expenditures

Total expenditures inside and outside the park

Question 26
For you and your personal group, please estimate all expenditures for the items listed below for this visit to Congaree NP and the surrounding area (within 1-hour drive of the park).

Results
- 63% of visitor groups spent $1-$200 (see Figure 62).

- 12% spent $201-$400.

- The average visitor group expenditure was $199.

- The median group expenditure (50% of groups spent more and 50% of groups spent less) was $55.

- The average total expenditure per person (per capita) was $106.

- As shown in Figure 63, the largest proportions of total expenditures inside and outside the park were:

  30% Lodges, hotels, motels, cabins, B&B, etc.
  21% Gas and oil
  19% Restaurants and bars
  12% All other purchases

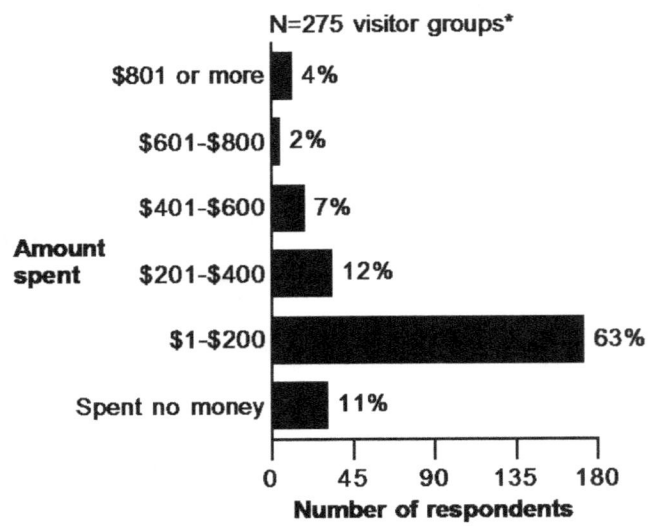

Figure 62. Total expenditures inside and outside the park

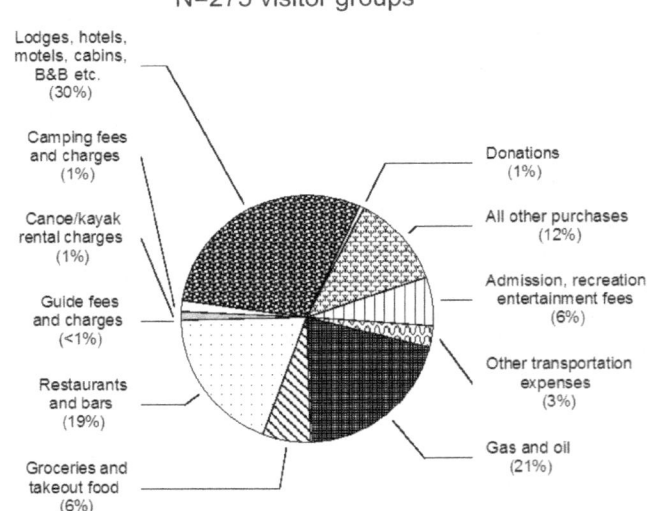

Figure 63. Proportions of total expenditures inside and outside the park

---

*total percentages do not equal 100 due to rounding
**total percentages do not equal 100 because visitors could select more than one answer

Number of adults covered by expenditures

Question 26c
How many adults (18 years or older)
do these expenses cover?

Results
- For 59% of visitor groups,
  expenditures covered two adults
  (see Figure 64).

- For 20%, expenditures covered
  one adult.

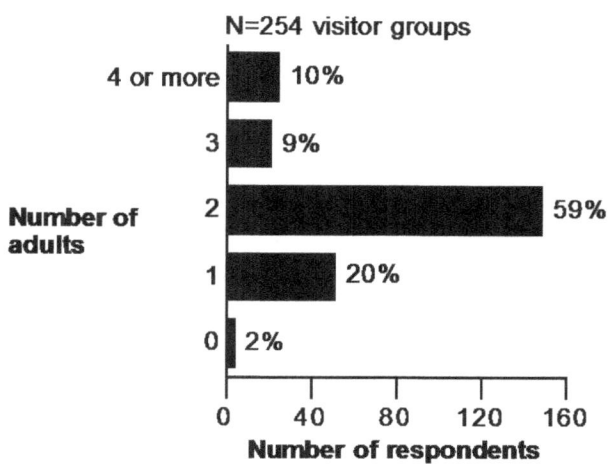

Figure 64. Number of adults covered by
expenditures

Number of children covered by expenditures

Question 26c
How many children (under 18 years)
do these expenses cover?

Results
- For 80% of visitor groups had no
  children covered by expenditures
  (see Figure 65).

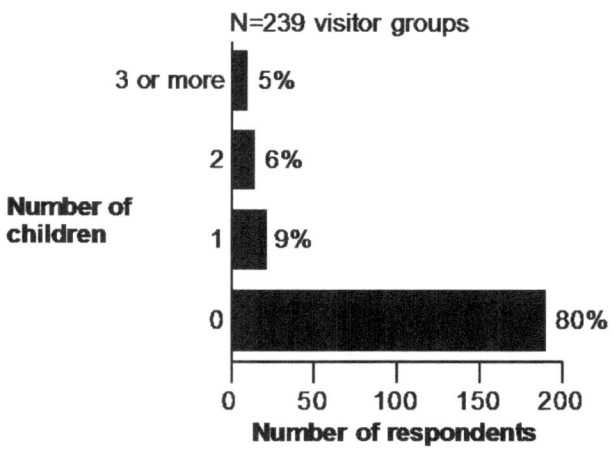

Figure 65. Number of children covered by
expenditures

---

*total percentages do not equal 100 due to rounding
**total percentages do not equal 100 because visitors could select more than one answer

Expenditures inside the park

Question 26a

Please list your personal group's total expenditures inside Congaree NP.

Results

- 48% of visitor groups spent no money inside the park (see Figure 66).

- 42% spent between $1 and $25.

- The average visitor group expenditure inside the park was $10.

- The median group expenditure (50% groups spent more and 50% of groups spent less) was $2.

- The average total expenditure per person (per capita) was $9.

- As shown in Figure 67, the largest proportion of total expenditures inside the park was:

    87% All other purchases

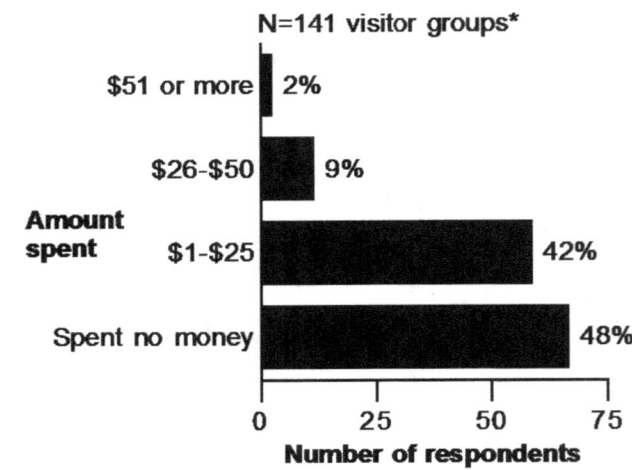

Figure 66. Total expenditures inside the park

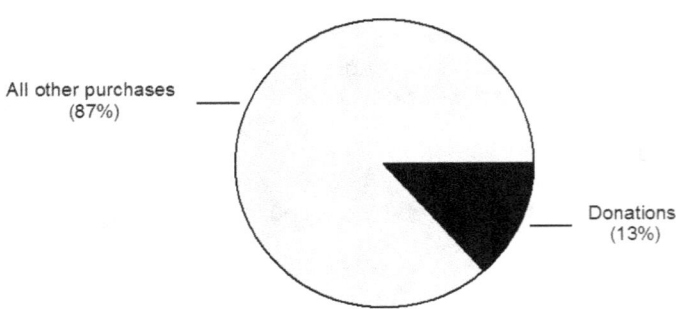

Figure 67. Proportions of total expenditures inside the park

_____

*total percentages do not equal 100 due to rounding
**total percentages do not equal 100 because visitors could select more than one answer

All other purchases (souvenirs, film, books, sporting goods, clothing, etc.)

- 52% of visitor groups spent no money on other purchases inside the park (see Figure 68).

- 24% spent $1-$10.

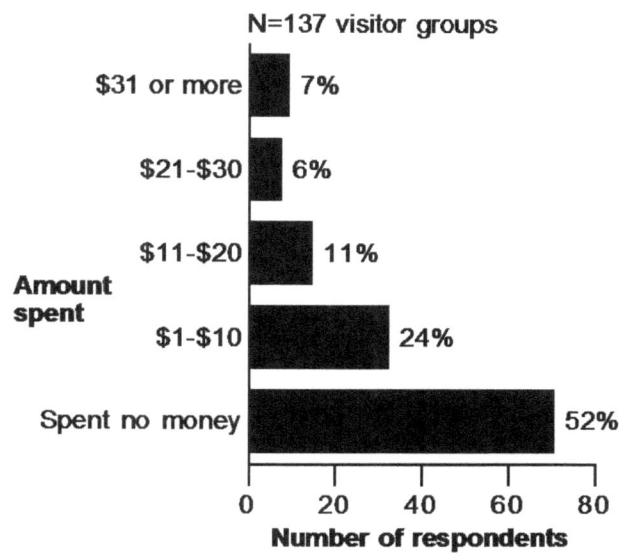

Figure 68. Expenditures for all other purchases inside the park

Donations

- 81% of visitor groups spent no money on donations inside the park (see Figure 69).

- 17% spent $1-$10.

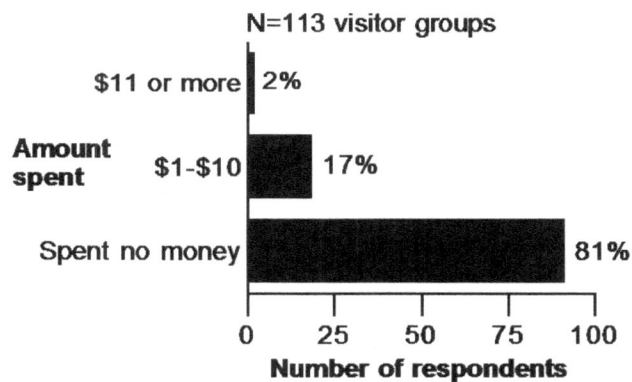

Figure 69. Expenditures for donations inside the park

*total percentages do not equal 100 due to rounding
**total percentages do not equal 100 because visitors could select more than one answer

Expenditures outside the park

Question 26b

Please list your group's total expenditures in the surrounding area outside the park (within 1-hour drive of park).

Results

- 61% of visitor groups spent $1-$200 (see Figure 70).

- 14% spent $401 or more.

- The average visitor group expenditure outside the park was $203.

- The median group expenditure (50% groups spent more and 50% of groups spent less) was $54.

- The average total expenditure per person (per capita) was $120.

- As shown in Figure 71, the largest proportions of total expenditures outside the park were:

  30% Lodges, hotels, motels, cabins, B&B, etc.
  21% Gas and oil
  20% Restaurants and bars

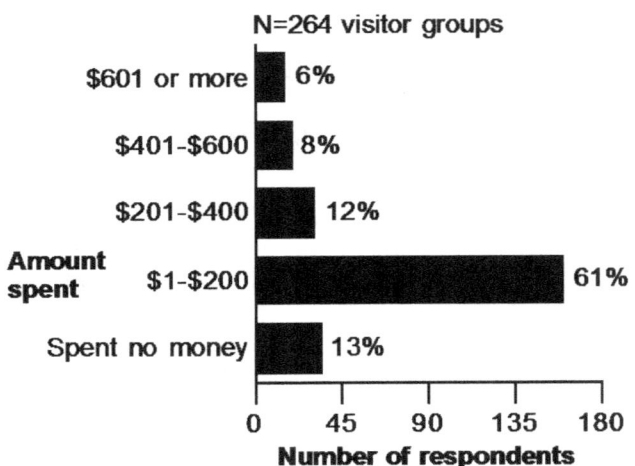

Figure 70. Total expenditures outside the park within 1-hour drive

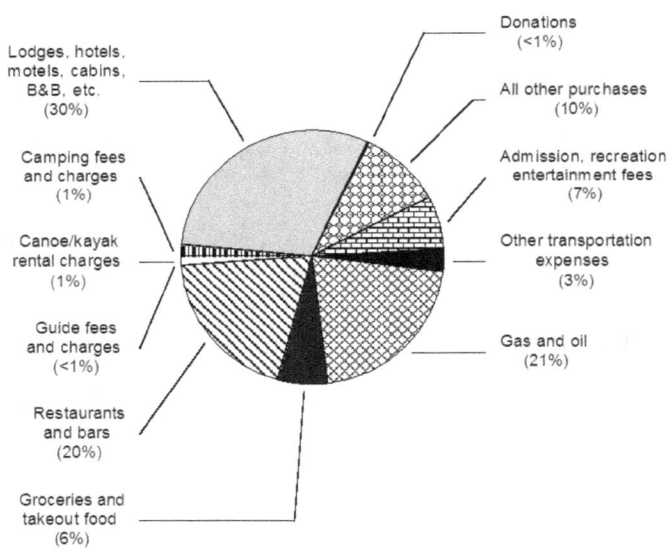

Figure 71. Proportions of total expenditures outside the park within 1-hour drive

---

*total percentages do not equal 100 due to rounding

**total percentages do not equal 100 because visitors could select more than one answer

Lodges, hotels, motels, cabins, B&B, etc.

- 63% of visitor groups spent no money on lodging outside the park (see Figure 72).
- 27% spent $1-$200.

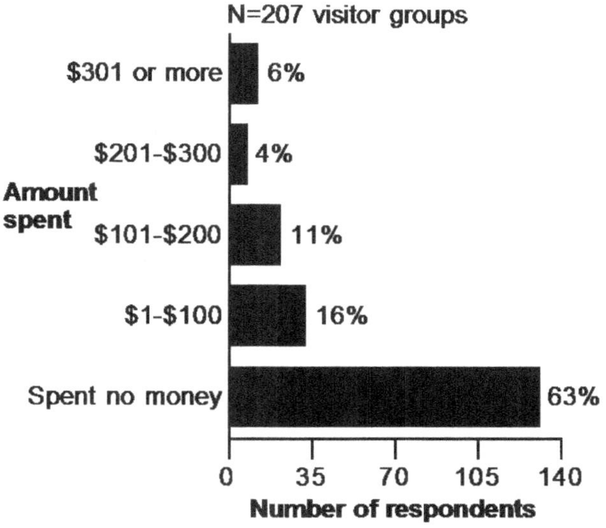

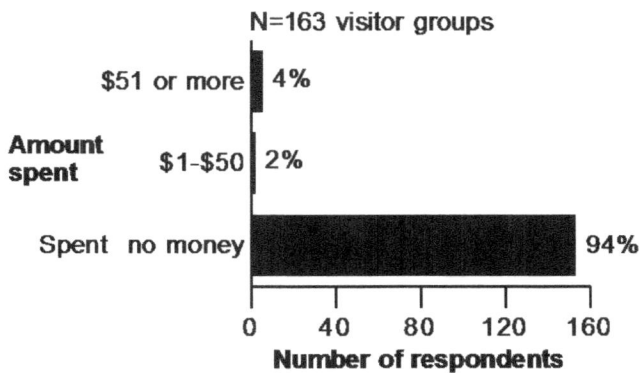

N=207 visitor groups
$301 or more
6%
$201-$300
4%
Amount spent
$101-$200
11%
$1-$100
16%
Spent no money
63%
0
35
70
105
140
Number of respondents

Figure 72. Expenditures for lodging outside the park

Camping fees and charges

- 94% of visitor groups spent no money on camping fees and charges outside the park (see Figure 73).

N=163 visitor groups
$51 or more
4%
Amount spent
$1-$50
2%
Spent no money
94%
0
40
80
120
160
Number of respondents

Figure 73. Expenditures for camping fees and charges outside the park

*total percentages do not equal 100 due to rounding
**total percentages do not equal 100 because visitors could select more than one answer

Canoe/kayak rental charges

- 97% of visitor groups spent no money on canoe/kayak rental charges outside the park (see Figure 74).

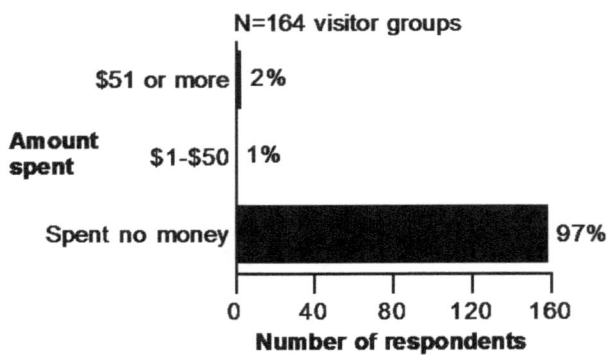

Figure 74. Expenditures for canoe/kayak rental charges outside the park

Guide fees and charges

- 99% of visitor groups spent no money on guide fees and charges outside the park (see Figure 75).

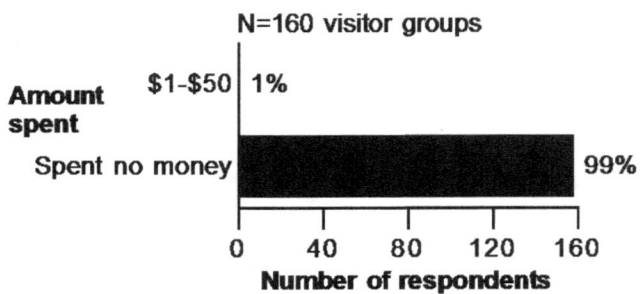

Figure 75. Expenditures for guide fees and charges outside the park

Restaurants and bars

- 45% of visitor groups spent no money on restaurants and bars outside the park (see Figure 76).

- 34% spent $1-$50.

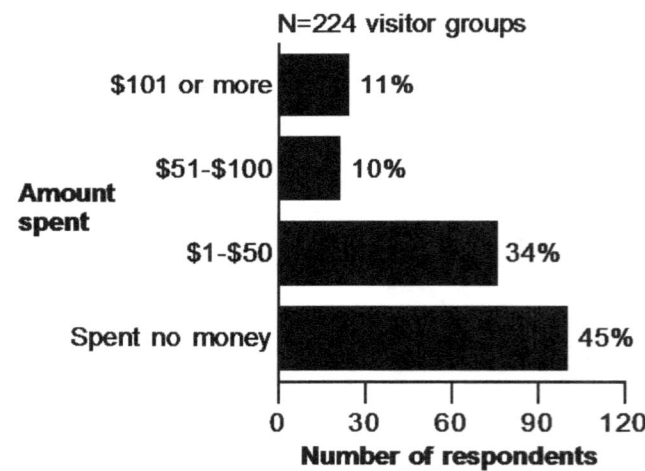

Figure 76. Expenditures for restaurants and bars outside the park

---

*total percentages do not equal 100 due to rounding
**total percentages do not equal 100 because visitors could select more than one answer

Groceries and takeout food

- 54% of visitor groups spent no money on groceries and takeout food outside the park (see Figure 77).

- 39% spent $1-$50.

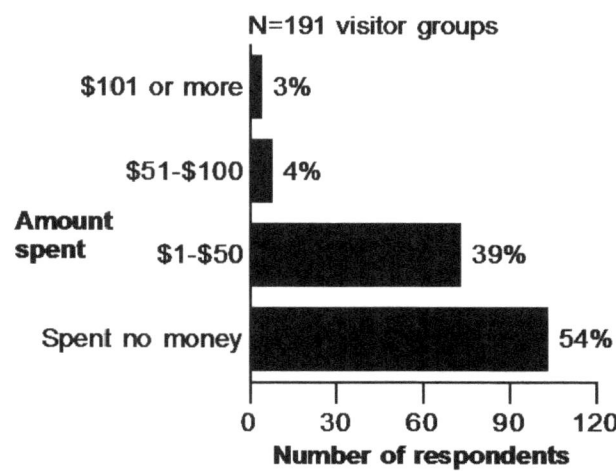

Figure 77. Expenditures for groceries and takeout food outside the park

Gas and oil (auto, RV, boat, etc.)

- 60% of visitor groups spent $1-$50 on gas and oil outside the park (see Figure 78).

- 18% spent no money.

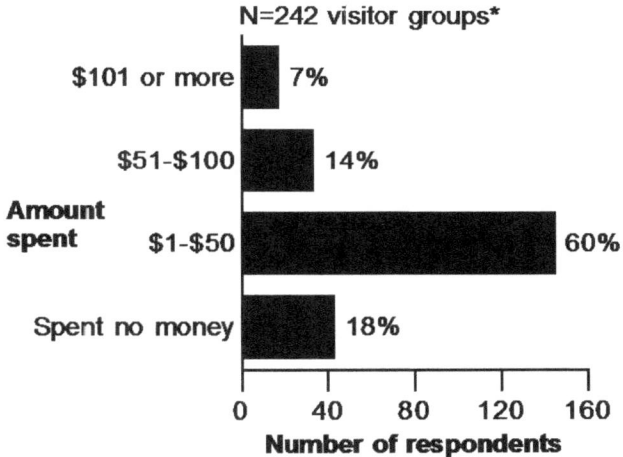

Figure 78. Expenditures for gas and oil outside the park

---

*total percentages do not equal 100 due to rounding
**total percentages do not equal 100 because visitors could select more than one answer

Other transportation (rental cars, taxis, auto repairs, but NOT airfare)

- 91% of visitor groups spent no money on other transportation outside the park (see Figure 79).

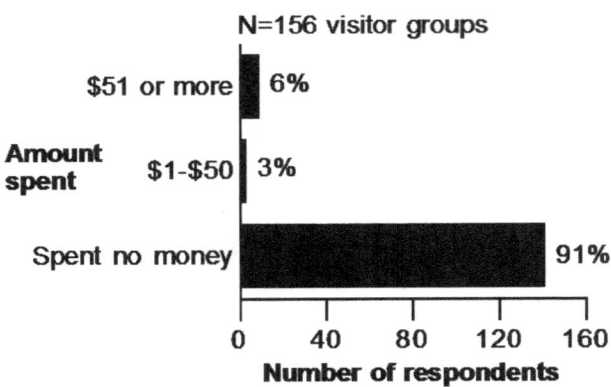

N=156 visitor groups

Figure 79. Expenditures for other transportation outside the park

Admission fees

- 89% of visitor groups spent no money on admission, recreation and entertainment fees (see Figure 80).

- 9% spent $1-$50.

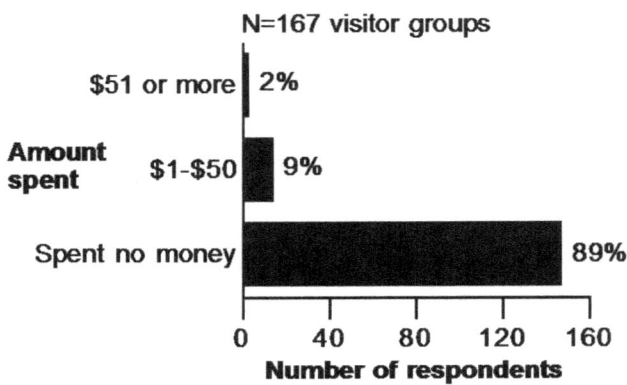

N=167 visitor groups

Figure 80. Expenditures for admission, recreation, entertainment fees outside the park

---

*total percentages do not equal 100 due to rounding
**total percentages do not equal 100 because visitors could select more than one answer

<u>All other purchases</u> (souvenirs, film, books, sporting goods, clothing, etc.)

- 71% of visitor groups spent no money on all other purchases outside the park (see Figure 81).

- 21% spent $1-$50.

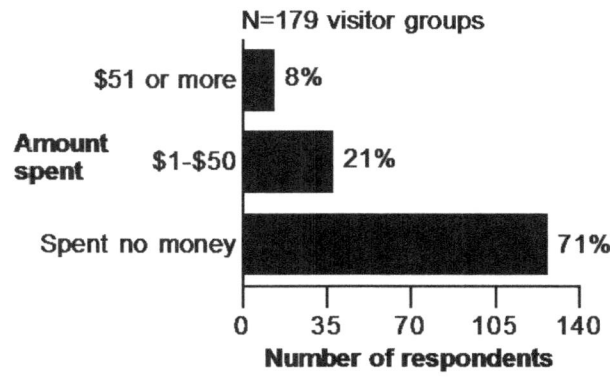

Figure 81. Expenditures for all other purchases outside the park

<u>Donations</u>

- 94% of visitor groups spent no money on donations outside the park (see Figure 82).

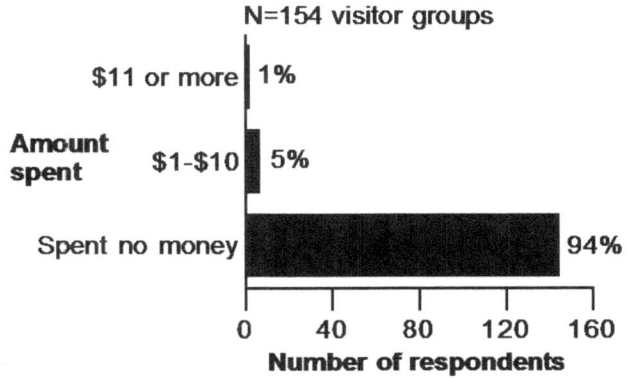

Figure 82. Expenditures for donations outside the park

Unpaid vacation/unpaid time off

Question 25c
  Did your household take any unpaid vacation or take unpaid time off of work to come on this trip?

Results
- 12% of visitor groups took unpaid vacation or time off work to come on this trip (see Figure 83).

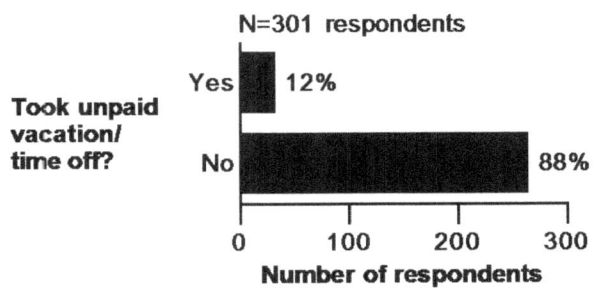

Figure 83. Unpaid vacation/time off used to make trip

---

*total percentages do not equal 100 due to rounding
**total percentages do not equal 100 because visitors could select more than one answer

Preferences for Future Visits

Likelihood to return to park in future

Question 28

Would you and your group be likely to visit Congaree NP again in the future?

Results

- 75% of visitor groups indicated that they would be likely to visit Congaree again in the future (see Figure 84).

- 17% of visitor groups were not sure about visiting the park in the future.

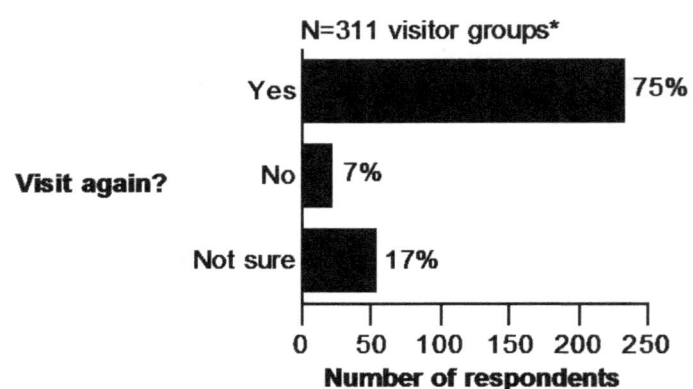

Figure 84. Visitor groups that would likely return to Congaree NP in the future

---

*total percentages do not equal 100 due to rounding
**total percentages do not equal 100 because visitors could select more than one answer

Preferred activities and programs on future visits

Question 30

If you were to visit Congaree NP in the future, which types of organized activities and programs would you and your personal group like to have available?

Results

- 75% of visitor groups were interested in attending organized activities or programs on a future visit to the park (see Figure 85).

- As shown in Figure 86, of those visitor groups that wanted organized activities/programs, the most preferred were:

    59% Canoeing/ kayaking
    50% Bird walks
    49% Owl prowls

- "Other" activities/programs (3%) were:

    Canoe shuttle
    Fishing
    Hunting to manage hogs
    Pig tours
    Plant identification

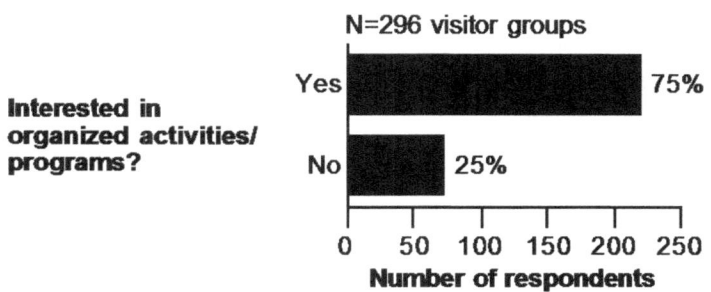

Figure 85. Interested in activities and programs

Figure 86. Preferred activities and programs

*total percentages do not equal 100 due to rounding
**total percentages do not equal 100 because visitors could select more than one answer

Preferred topics to learn on future visit

Question 31

If you were to visit Congaree NP in the future, which subjects would you and your personal group like to learn more about?

Results

- 88% of visitor groups were interested in learning about the park on future visits (see Figure 87).

- As shown in Figure 88, of those visitor groups that were interested in learning about the park, the most common topics were:

  70% Plants/animals
  57% Old growth
       floodplain forest
  56% Champion trees
  54% History

- "Other" topics (1%) were:

  Cabins for overnight visits
  Everything
  Pigs (big ones)
  Walks

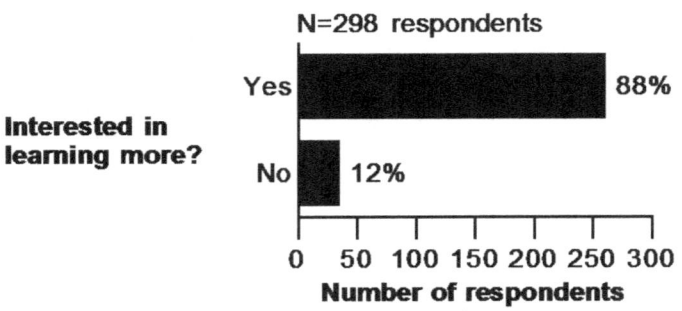

Figure 87. Visitor groups that were interested in learning more about the park

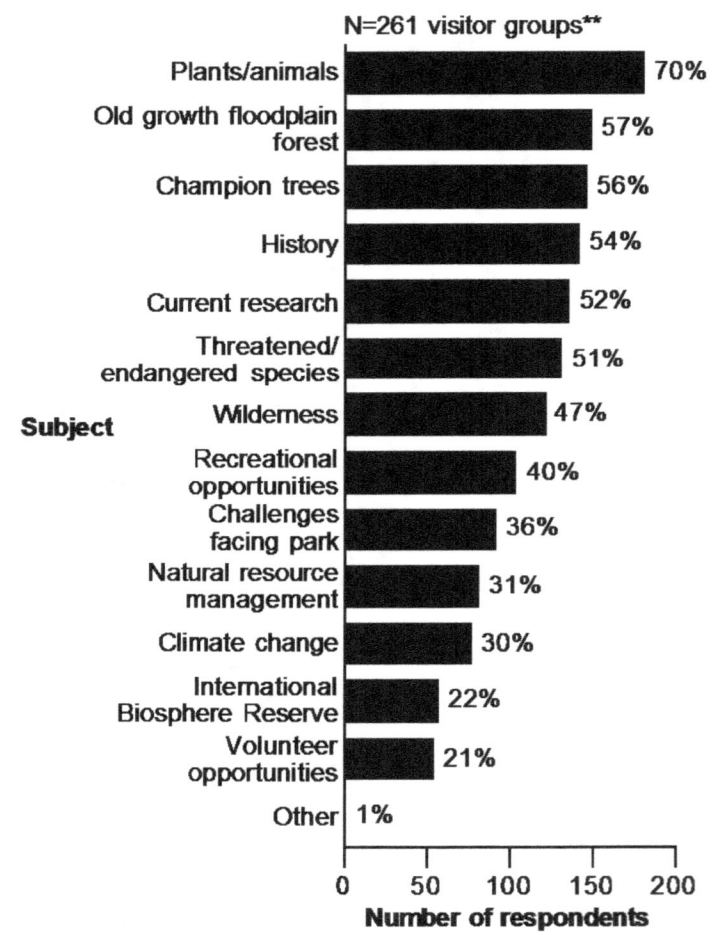

Figure 88. Subjects to learn on future visit

---

*total percentages do not equal 100 due to rounding
**total percentages do not equal 100 because visitors could select more than one answer

Overall Quality

Quality of facilities, services and recreational opportunities

Question 27

Overall, how would you rate the quality of facilities, services, and recreational opportunities provided to you and your personal group at Congaree NP during this visit?

Results

- 95% of visitor groups rated the overall quality of facilities, services, and recreational opportunities as "very good" or "good" (see Figure 89).

- 1% of visitor groups rated the quality as "poor."

- No visitor groups rated the quality as "very poor."

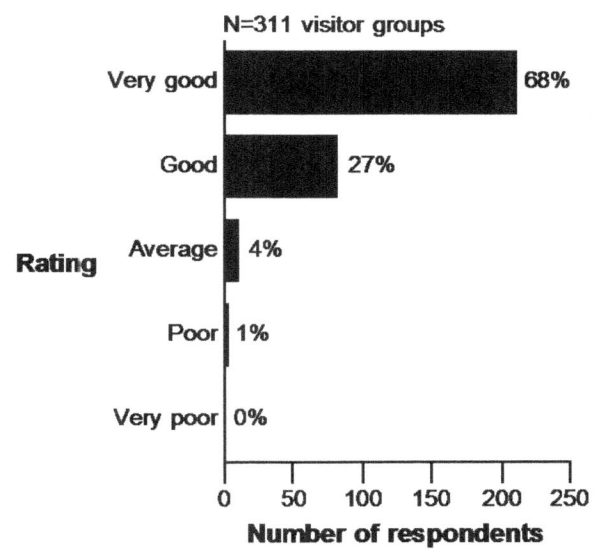

Figure 89. Overall quality rating of facilities, services, and recreational opportunities

*total percentages do not equal 100 due to rounding
**total percentages do not equal 100 because visitors could select more than one answer

Visitor Comment Summaries

What visitors liked most

Question 32a
What did you and your personal group like most about your visit to Congaree NP? (Open-ended)

Results

- 88% of visitor groups (N=276) responded to this question.

- Table 20 shows a summary of visitor comments. A copy of hand-written comments can be found in the Visitor Comments section.

Table 20. What visitors liked most
(N=446 comments; some visitor groups made more than one comment.)

Comment	Number of times mentioned
PERSONNEL (3%)	
Rangers/park staff	6
Helpful staff	4
Friendly rangers	3
INTERPRETIVE SERVICES (9%)	
Trail guide brochure	7
Guided canoe tour	5
Exhibits	5
Visitor center	3
Learning about trees	3
Learning about history	2
Learning about the park	2
Mosquito meter	2
Other comments	9
FACILITIES/MAINTENANCE (22%)	
Boardwalk	59
Trails	18
Clean trails	4
Cleanliness of park	3
Campground	2
Trail signs	2
Backcountry experiences	2
Other comments	7
POLICY/MANAGEMENT (3%)	
Uncrowded	9
Other comments	4

Table 20. What visitors liked most (continued)

Comment	Number of times mentioned
RESOURCE MANAGEMENT (26%)	
Trees	22
Animals/wildlife	20
Giant trees	13
Wildlife observation	9
Plants	8
Old growth forest	7
Bird sightings/watching	5
Bird sounds/songs	4
Birds	4
Cypress trees	4
Natural diversity	4
Turtles	3
Seeing pileated woodpeckers	2
Seeing wild pigs	2
Other comments	10
GENERAL (38%)	
Quietness/peacefulness	43
Nature	25
Solitude	16
Beauty/beautiful park	13
Scenery	10
Atmosphere - clean/fresh	5
The swamp	5
Walking/hiking	5
Forest sounds	4
Different ecosystem	3
Beautiful scenery	2
Canoeing on Cedar Creek	2
Everything	2
Family activity	2
Fishing	2
Park is close to home	2
The forest	2
Unique environment	2
Weather	2
Wilderness	2
Other comments	19

What visitors liked least

Question 32b

What did you and your personal group like least about your visit to Congaree NP? (Open-ended)

Results

- 64% of visitor groups (N=201) responded to this question.

- Table 21 shows a summary of visitor comments. A copy of hand-written comments can be found in the Visitor Comments section.

Table 21. What visitors liked least
(N=210 comments; some visitor groups made more than one comment.)

Comment	Number of times mentioned
INTERPRETIVE SERVICES (5%)	
No signs identifying plants	2
Other comments	8
FACILITIES/MAINTENANCE (15%)	
Lack of directional signs to park	8
Fallen trees on trail	2
Inadequate signage for park on Bluff Road from Columbia	2
Litter	2
No after hours restroom facilities	2
Trail distances not clear on signage	2
Trail markers lacking at some intersections	2
Other comments	11
POLICY/MANAGEMENT (14%)	
Noisy school groups	5
Aircraft noise	4
Loud talking on trails	4
Bikes on boardwalk	2
The survey	2
Train noise	2
Other comments	10
RESOURCE MANAGEMENT (49%)	
Mosquitos	88
Insects	6
Pig damage to forest	3
Snakes	3
Other comments	3
GENERAL (18%)	
Nothing to dislike	16
Rain	3
Heat	2
Humidity	2
Not enough time	2
Other comments	12

Significance of the park

Question 33

Congaree NP was established because of its significance to the nation. In your opinion, what is the national significance of this park? (Open-ended)

Results

- 76% of visitor groups (N=237) responded to this question.

- Table 22 shows a summary of visitor comments. A copy of hand-written comments can be found in the Visitor Comments section.

Table 22. Significance of the park
(N=277 comments; some visitor groups made more than one comment)

Comment	Number of times mentioned
Preservation of bottomland old growth forest	38
Historic value/significance	15
Old growth forest	15
Large/old trees	14
Unique environment/habitat	14
Old growth forests are rare/vanishing	13
Important/significant	11
Natural beauty/setting	9
Old growth floodplain forest	9
Uniqueness	8
Beautiful place/park	7
Do not know	7
Educational value/significance	6
Nature preserved	6
Natural/pristine/untouched forest	5
Preserves an ecosystem/environment	5
Swamp	5
Biodiversity/species diversity	4
Champion trees	4
Historical preservation	4
Preservation of specific plant/animal species	4
Protected area in South Carolina	4
Wetlands are important	4
Wilderness is valuable	4
Wilderness preservation/protection	4
Wildlife sanctuary/protection	4
Example of lowland forest	3
Flora and fauna	3
Parks are important to protect wilderness	3
Bottomland floodplain	2
Educate future generations about biodiversity	2
For the benefit of future generations	2
Habitat preservation	2
Largest untouched forest	2
Southern swamp	2

Table 22. Significance of the park, (continued)

Comment	Number of times mentioned
To be protected	2
Unspoiled/untouched land	2
Variety of vegetation	2
Other comments	27

Planning for the future

Question 34

If you were a manager planning for the future of Congaree National Park, what would you and personal group propose? (Open-ended)

Results

- 58% of visitor groups (N=181) responded to this question.

- Table 23 shows a summary of visitor comments. A copy of hand-written comments can be found in the Visitor Comments section.

Table 23. Planning for the future
(N=235 comments; some visitor groups made more than one comment.)

Comment	Number of times mentioned
PERSONNEL (<1%)	
Comments	1
INTERPRETIVE SERVICES (21%)	
More ranger-guided canoe trips	5
Additional interpretive signs on trails	3
Family activities	3
More ranger-guided activities	3
More self-guided information	3
Educate the public about forest ecosystem	2
Emphasize uniqueness of Congaree	2
Improve park video	2
More information about plants and trees	2
Other comments	25
FACILITIES/MAINTENANCE (27%)	
Extended/additional boardwalks	12
More directional signs to the park	10
Expand trail system	8
Improve campground facilities	5
Backcountry campsites	4
Campsites for RVs	3
Access to wilderness areas/other park areas	2
Build aerial platforms for tree canopy observation	2
Easier/more fishing access	2
Expand camping facilities	2
Maintain trails	2
Improve trail signs	2
Other comments	10

Table 23. Planning for the future (continued)

Comment	Number of times mentioned
POLICY/MANAGEMENT (32%)	
Expand park boundaries	16
Publicize/educate the public about park/activities	14
Keep it as it is	12
Preserve/protect the park	9
Keep it natural	4
Publicize/educate locals about the park	4
Continue to protect the park/environment	2
Improve access	2
No development in immediate area	2
Shorter questionnaire	2
Other comments	8
RESOURCE MANAGEMENT (8%)	
Remove wild pigs	6
Control mosquitos	2
Protect upstream water quality	2
Other comments	8
CONCESSIONS (5%)	
Sell mosquito repellent	4
Food services	2
Other comments	5
GENERAL (6%)	
Keep up the good work/good job	9
Other comments	6

Additional comments

Question 35

Is there anything else you and your personal group would like to tell us about your visit to Congaree National Park? (Open-ended)

Results

- 46% of visitor groups (N=145) responded to this question.

- Table 24 shows a summary of visitor comments. A copy of hand-written comments can be found in the Visitor Comments section.

Table 24. Additional comments
(N=189 comments; some visitor groups made more than one comment.)

Comment	Number of times mentioned
PERSONNEL (12%)	
Staff was helpful	7
Staff was great/nice	5
Staff was friendly	5
Staff was knowledgeable/professional	3
Other comments	2
INTERPRETIVE SERVICES (7%)	
Enjoy ranger-led activities	2
Other comments	10
FACILITIES/MAINTENANCE (12%)	
Improve signage to the park	9
Enjoyed boardwalk	3
Facilities nice/well maintained	3
Other comments	9
POLICY/MANAGEMENT (6%)	
Charge entrance fee	2
Other comments	9
RESOURCE MANAGEMENT (4%)	
Too many mosquitos	4
Other comments	4
CONCESSIONS (1%)	
Comments	2

Table 24. Additional comments (continued)

Comment	Number of times mentioned
GENERAL (58%)	
Enjoyed visit	34
Will return	17
Love the park	11
Thank you	10
Keep up the good work	8
Great park/place	6
Beautiful park	5
Park is a treasure	3
Park is accessible	2
Thankful for efforts to create and preserve park	2
Visit regularly	2
Other comments	10

Visitor Comments

This section contains visitor responses to open-ended questions.

Appendix 1: The Questionnaire

Appendix 2: Additional Analysis

The Visitor Services Project (VSP) offers the opportunity to learn from VSP visitor study data through additional analysis. Two-way and three-way cross tabulations can be made with any questions.

Below are some examples of the types of cross tabulations that can be requested. To make a request, please use the contact information below, and include your name, address and phone number in the request.

1. What proportion of family groups with children attend interpretive programs?

2. Is there a correlation between visitors' ages and their preferred sources of information about the park?

3. Are highly satisfied visitors more likely to return for a future visit?

4. How many international visitors participate in hiking?

5. What ages of visitors would use the park website as a source of information on a future visit?

6. Is there a correlation between visitor groups' rating of the overall quality of their park experience and their ratings of individual services and facilities?

7. Do larger visitor groups (e.g., four or more) participate in different activities than smaller groups?

8. Do frequent visitors rate the overall quality of their park experiences differently than less frequent visitors?

The VSP database website (http://vsp.uidaho.edu) allows data searches for comparisons of data from one or more parks.

For more information please contact:

Visitor Services Project, PSU
College of Natural Resources
P.O. Box 441139
University of Idaho
Moscow, ID 83843-1139

Phone: 208-885-2585
Fax: 208-885-4261
Email: lenale@uidaho.edu
Website: http://www.psu.uidaho.edu

Appendix 3: Decision Rules for Checking Non-response Bias

There are several methods for checking non-response bias. However, the most common way is to use some demographic indicators to compare between respondents and non-respondents (Dey 1997; Salant and Dillman 1994; Dillman and Carley-Baxter 2000; Dillman, 2007; Stoop 2004). In this study, we used five variable group type, group size, age of the group member (at least 16 years old) completing the survey, whether the park was the primary destination for the visit, and visitor's place of residence proximity to the park to check for non-response bias.

A Chi-square tests were used to detect the difference in the response rates among different group types, whether the park was the primary destination for this visit, and visitor's place of residence and proximity to the park. The hypothesis was that there is no significant difference across different categories (or groups) between respondents and non-respondents. If the p-value is greater than 0.05, the difference between respondents and non-respondents is judged to be insignificant.

Two independent-sample T-tests were used to test the differences between respondent's and non-respondent's average age and group size. The p-values represent the significance levels of these tests. If p-value is greater than 0.05, the two groups are judged to be insignificantly different.

Therefore, the hypotheses for checking non-response bias are:

1. Respondents from different group types are equally represented

2. Respondents and non-respondents are not significantly different in term of proximity from their home to the park

3. Respondents and non-respondents are not significantly different in term of reason for visiting the park

4. Average age of respondents – average age of non-respondents = 0

5. Average group size of respondents – average group size of non-respondents = 0

As shown in Tables 3, 4, 5 and 6, the p-value for respondent/non-respondent comparisons are less than 0.05, indicating significant differences between respondents and non-respondents. The results indicate some biases occurred due to nonresponse. Visitors at younger age ranges (especially 40 and younger), came from the local area (within a 50 mile radius), and visitors traveling with friends were underrepresented in the survey results. Results of the study in this report only reflect the simple frequencies. Inferences of the survey results should be weighted to counter balance the effects of nonresponse bias.

References

Dey, E. L. (1997). Working with Low Survey Response Rates: The Efficacy of Weighting Adjustment. *Research in Higher Education*, 38(2): 215-227.

Dillman, D. A. (2007). *Mail and Internet Surveys: The Tailored Design Method, Updated version with New Internet, Visual, and Mixed-Mode Guide*, 2nd Edition, New York: John Wiley and Sons, Inc.

Dillman, D. A. and Carley-Baxter, L. R. (2000). *Structural determinants of survey response rate over a 12-year period, 1988-1999*, Proceedings of the section on survey research methods, 394-399, American Statistical Association, Washington, DC.

Filion, F. L. (Winter 1975-Winter 1976). Estimating Bias due to Non-response in Mail Surveys. *Public Opinion Quarterly*, Vol 39 (4): 482-492.

Goudy, W. J. (1976). Non-response Effect on Relationships Between Variables. *Public Opinion Quarterly*. Vol 40 (3): 360-369.

Mayer, C. S. and Pratt Jr. R. W. (Winter 1966-Winter 1967). A Note on Non-response in a Mail Survey. *Public Opinion Quarterly*. Vol 30 (4): 637-646.

Salant, P. and Dillman, D. A. (1994). *How to Conduct Your Own Survey*. U.S.: John Wiley and Sons, Inc.

Stoop, I. A. L. (2004). Surveying Non-respondents. *Field Methods*, 16 (1): 23.

NPS 178/112717 . February 2012

www.ingramcontent.com/pod-product-compliance
Lightning Source LLC
Chambersburg PA
CBHW081118290526
45795CB00006B/2164